RUSTIC GARDEN PROJECTS

28 Decorative Accents You Can Build

Dawn King

Creative Publishing
international

CHANHASSEN, MINNESOTA
www.creativepub.com

Creative Publishing international

Copyright © 2006 by Creative Publishing international, Inc.
18705 Lake Drive East
Chanhassen, MN 55317
1-800-328-3895
www.creativepub.com

President/CEO: Ken Fund
Vice President/Publisher: Linda Ball
Vice President/Retail Sales & Marketing: Kevin Haas

Author: Dawn King
Executive Editor, Home Improvement: Bryan Trandem
Editor: Jerri Farris
Art Director: Jon Simpson
Book Designer: Kari Johnston
Assistant Managing Editor: Tracy Stanley
Production Manager: Linda Halls
Illustrator: Isaiah King
Photographer: Christa Matthews

Printed in China
10 9 8 7 6 5 4 3 2 1

Contents

RUSTIC GARDEN PROJECTS
by Dawn King
All photographs copyright © 2006 Christa Matthews
except Front Cover (large); © 2006 Creative Publishing
international
All Illustrations © Isaiah King

Library of Congress Cataloging-in-Publication Data

King, Dawn, 1946-
  Rustic garden projects : 18 decorative accents you can build /
by Dawn King.
      p. cm.
  Includes bibliographical references and index.
  ISBN 1-58923-155-4 (soft cover : alk. paper)
1. Garden ornaments and furniture--Design and construction.
2. Garden structures--Design and construction. I. Title.
  SB473.5.K56 2006
  684.1'8--dc22   2005026210

Introduction

Creating things from natural materials has always been central to my life. As a child, I spent much time out-of-doors, exploring wooded areas near our homes or camping with my family. My mother was artistic and always involved in making things. Fascinated with how things were done in the pioneer days, she introduced us to weaving cattail fronds on hanging looms such as the Native Americans used, and one summer she even made a coracle— a small boat built from a bowl-shaped twig frame with a leather covering.

My mother was handy with many things, and along with my father, we helped build a lean-to campsite, lashing poles together to make a ladder for the loft of the structure. For a neighboring camp, we built an Iroquois longhouse with bent saplings. Early on in my life, I grew comfortable with taking materials from the woods and fashioning them into whatever was needed.

As an adult, attempting to make a living while staying at home with my children, I turned to art in various forms. I sewed clothing and quilts, copper enameled jewelry and small household items, worked for a sheepskin company making their jackets and coats, and wove baskets. The baskets slowly evolved into larger and larger projects. Eventually my neighbor, Ineke deVries, taught me to make a child's chair. It was a small project, but one that required new skills (and different muscles) than I had used before. With the help of talented neighbors, many of whom have built their own homes and some of whom are professional woodworkers or carpenters, I began to develop my carpentry skills and soon found that my trellises and arbors had new sturdiness and durability. No longer did they wobble or fall apart.

I kept asking questions, trying new things, and came up with the many designs which can be found in this book. Some of the designs, the chair in particular, are traditional ones which have been adapted to the particular materials I use. Others have evolved from suggestions of friends, students, and customers who had ideas of their own and only needed my help to manifest them.

☙ This ensemble setting features a garden sofa (page 123) and a coffee table (page 102). At the peak of the shed in the background, you'll see a star (page 34). The arbor structure shown here is not one of my designs, but it demonstrates how creative my students can be.

As I progressed in my own work, I began to teach others. At first it was day-long workshops at home or at Rideau Nursery in North Gower, Ontario. I then designed several series of night classes for the local community college. You will find that the projects found in the opening pages of the book will go quickly. Many will take half a day or less, and the chair, arbor and garden bench will probably take a day.

This book has grown out of the notes I've created to help my students in their own work. Many of these students have gone well beyond my basic instructions and created designs of their own. You will see photos of several students' work in the pages of this book. I am always excited and inspired when someone veers away from my basic instruction and creates a new design. It inspires me to expand my own ideas, which tend towards the symmetrical and confined. I encourage you to explore variations to the projects I've included here and not feel compelled to make them look exactly like mine.

You will not need to be an experienced woodworker to do the projects in this book. If you are using a power drill and particularly a chop saw, it would be helpful to have someone knowledgeable instruct you, but the skills are easy to master. In my experience, women in particular are intimidated by power tools or even by the thought of building something on their own. I especially love to teach women who are doing these things for the first time. Halfway into the class, they discover an ease with the tools, and by the end they have produced a lovely product made by their own labor and creativity. Their excitement is contagious, as it will be for you, too.

If you are already familiar with using tools and working with wood, you will find these projects straightforward. If this is your first time working with trees and branches, as opposed to milled lumber, it may be a bit more challenging. It is hard to be precise with curved and bumpy wood, so you will need to be flexible in your expectations. If you find yourself fretting over a project that is not "perfect," you have the option of either correcting it or accepting it as is. I remind you, as I do my other students, that this is not fine woodworking. Do the best you can, but realize that you're working with natural products that have their quirks. The goal is to have a good time and to create a beautiful, useful piece at the end of the day. Some of the most interesting projects come about when things don't go exactly as planned.

I hope you enjoy these projects as much as we have and that you go on to make many of your own. I intend this book to be a starting point for you. When you have mastered the basic techniques, be creative and explore different ideas. Appreciate the beauty of the wood with which you are working and the piece you are creating, and most important, have a good time. ❧

❧ Author Dawn King at Kiwi Gardens,
(Perth, Ontario) near her home

❧ Rustic garden furniture works well in ensembles of several pieces. In my yard, I've grouped two chairs and a sofa variation to create an outdoor sitting room beneath my flowering crab apple tree. The rustic fence you see is 8 ft. high to keep deer out of my garden. You'll find directions for building a chair like this on page 116.

↬ (top) The furniture plans you find in this book can be easily adapted to different sizes. I took the same basic designs seen on the opposite page and down-sized them to make a wee-sized furniture ensemble for children. The actors in this drama are Oliver, the son of our photographer, Christa Matthews; and my nieces, Katie and Julia Bowles. Directions for the chairs and sofa begin on page 116; for the cedar table, page 106.

↬ (above left) Branches with stripped bark can also make fine garden pieces. This chair is made from branches deformed into interesting shapes by vines. These wood pieces came from Ohio, and became barkless when customs officers at the Canadian border insisted that the bark be stripped off.

↬ (above right) A garden shelf is an ideal place to display decorative pottery, metal work, or flower arrangements. This is a piece I built; the decorative branches are red dogwood. It currently resides in the garden of Lynda Jenkins. See page 94 to build a garden shelf like this one.

ꙮ (above left) A decorative fence creates interesting patterns in the garden of Denyse Marion-Barrie, one of my most talented students. Every fence is different; learn a basic method for fence building on page 72.

ꙮ (above right) This delightful ensemble is in the garden of Andy Fisher and Jill Dunkley. The garden bench shown here is a variation of the plan found on page 110; the tripod birdbath is an adaptation of the tripod planter found on page 40. The driftwood fan trellis is the creation of Scott Dobson.

ꙮ (right) Many rustic pieces are more than just decoration. These obelisks provide the framework for climbing vegetables in the garden of Denyse Marion-Barrie. Learn how to build these on page 62. The fence in the background is a marvelous 100-ft. long creation, with each panel entirely unique.

᭏ (left) One of our local businesses, Rideau Nursery, both sells my furniture pieces and uses them to display plants for sale. This rustic couch, a variation of the garden chair project on page 116, could also be used to display potted plants in your own garden.

᭏ (below) Friends of mine, Donna Dolan and Cathy Wilson, created this wholly unique design for a small bridge, using nothing more than the joinery techniques you'll learn on the following pages. One of the joys of rustic construction is making creations that are entirely your own.

❧ (above) A basic garden bench (page 110) with strong geometric shapes and a simple cedar table (page 106) make a delightful grouping on this small patio belonging to Jeff and Chantalle Woodrow, of Ottowa, Ontario. Rustic pieces fit in well in almost any surrounding.

❧ (right) This garden bench variation is a natural in a pioneer setting, where the buildings, fencing, and other accessories are all period in style.

❧ Here's another rustic furniture ensemble from my workshop, this one featuring two garden chairs, a sofa variation, and a coffee table. Directions for the chairs and sofa can be found on page 116; the coffee table is a slight variation from the plan on page 102.

❧ (above left) All sorts of materials can be incorporated into rustic furniture projects. Polished stones are attached to this tabletop.

❧ (above right) Ceramic tile is a natural—and colorful— fit for a rustic table.

❧ Another talented artist, Ineke deVries, designed and built these pieces. The bench is constructed of barn wood with melted glass. The end table is made from willow.

❧ (above) These end tables are also the creation of artist Ineke deVries.

❧ (top) In this scene, the long planter (page 68) accompanies a classic arbor (page 80). These are from the garden of Lynda Jenkins.

❧ (below) Another scene from my own garden: these are down-sized pieces designed for children. The sofa is a scaled-down version of the bench variation on page 123; the cedar table is a downsized model of the project on page 106. Nearly any of the plans in this book can be scaled to different sizes.

Tools

The tools needed for rustic work are very simple. You can manage with a sharp bypass pruning shears, a hammer, a saw, and a drill.

Many people make their furniture using hammers and nails, I use drills and screws for all but the small, decorative pieces. When using screws, it is handy to have at least two drills—one for drilling pilot holes and one for driving screws. I find corded drills are best for drilling as they tend to have more power and speed. A 12- or 14.4-volt cordless drill is excellent for driving screws. When purchasing a cordless drill, make sure the weight is comfortable, and make sure there are two batteries so you can continue your work with one while the other is being recharged.

When screwing together larger pieces, I use decking screws. I prefer screws with square-drive heads, but Phillips heads will also work. For smaller work (e.g., tables, planters) drywall screws are my favorite. They use Phillips bits, and come in a variety of sizes.

My older son, who is a carpenter and contractor, introduced me to drywall trim screws. Although they are made of a softer metal and strip more easily, I sometimes use them when I am doing a fancier piece and don't want the screw to show as much. Again, I prefer the square-headed screws to the Phillips.

When decorating with finer pieces of wood, there are many options available. To attach decorative pieces to the framework, you can use either screws or nails. Spiral nails and ring nails will hold better than common (smooth-shanked) nails, especially in a situation where there is tension on the wood. Staples can also be used to fasten branches to larger support pieces. I sometimes use a medium-sized version of fencing staples, which are quite substantial. I also use U-shaped, double-sided tacks that are similar in shape but even smaller. One of my handiest tools is a staplegun that has rounded staples. On occasion, I wire two pieces together, usually in places where it would be awkward to drill pilot holes or where the pieces are too fine to attach in any other way. When this is necessary, such as when attaching an angel's halo (page 66), I use a fine wire that is nearly invisible.

When I first began making trellises and arbors, I cut my stock using a hand saw, but these days I use an electric miter saw (sometimes called a

≈ You can make just about every project in this book with this basic tool set, which includes (clockwise from top left) a power drill, a stapler, a cordless drill, a bypass pruning shears, a pruning saw, and a hammer. Once you get the fever, though, you may find additional tools helpful (opposite page).

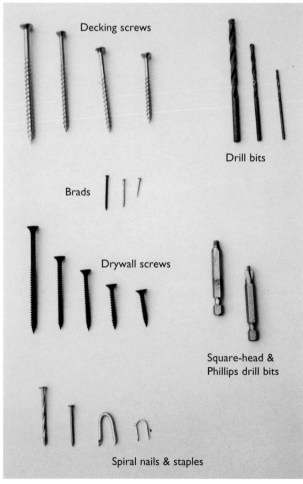

Decking screws

Drill bits

Brads

Drywall screws

Square-head &
Phillips drill bits

Spiral nails & staples

❧ These tools will be helpful for serious hobbyists (clockwise from top left): protective helmet with ear protection, eye protectors, utility knife, chisel, angle grinder, spade bits, ratcheted shears with extendable handle, chain saw.

"chop saw") and can't really imagine using anything else. You don't need a fancy, compound miter saw. You will being doing mostly straight cuts, and occasionally a simple angle, so a very basic saw will do. Do make sure, though, that the saw has an effective safety guard on the blade.

A small chain saw also can be useful, especially if you make many projects. Used carefully, it can be a true time-saver. Another tool that may be helpful is a rotary grinder equipped with a Kutzall disc for sculpting. This is a tool that requires instruction and practice to use well. With the saws and the angle grinder, ear and eye protection is a necessity. And if you are sensitive to dust, it is good to use a dust mask when cutting.

Make sure to use the appropriate tools for the job, keep them in good condition, and work at angles and heights that are the most efficient and comfortable. If you find your wrists, arms, and shoulders getting tired, try to find a better position. The height of your worktables should be adjusted to suit your height whenever possible.

Joinery Techniques

∾ This is my workshop near Perth, Ontario. Building rustic furniture and ornaments doesn't require a lot of tools, but a large, flat worksurface is a must.

By their nature, rustic projects will require "rustic" joinery techniques. Don't expect to get the kind of perfect, tight-fitting joints used in fine woodworking. There are three basic joining techniques that I use:

Most commonly, I use what I call "face joints." This is fastening one piece of wood directly on top of another. At the juncture of the two, I drill two pilot holes as far apart from each other as possible in the allotted space. I put a nail or screw into one hole to hold the two pieces together while other joints are made. When all joints have one screw in them, I make sure the pieces are exactly where they should be, and everything is squared up. Then I secure the shape by putting in the second nail or screw.

∾ When assembling a piece of furniture, it is important to prevent racking, or twisting. This is usually done with triangular bracing of some sort. This bracing can be done with a forked branch or a straight branch appropriately placed, joining the upright piece of your framework to the crosspiece of your framework. You may have to place one in each direction to secure the shape of your piece and give it strength. When putting pressure on it from all directions, the joint should not move at all. Often your decorations will supply this bracing.

These techniques are described within the project instructions. However, as you begin to design your own pieces, these are the principles that you need to keep in mind.

Mortise and tenon techniques provide strong, sturdy joints, but they are definitely more challenging. A hole, called a mortise, is drilled using a large bit—a spade bit works well—into the main piece of wood. (This is usually a chair or bench leg or a bed post.) Then the crosspiece is either inserted directly into this hole or is cut down to the appropriate size to fit into the hole. This can be done by hand with a sharp knife or with a tool called a tenon cutter. A tenon cutter fits onto a drill and is somewhat like a large pencil sharpener. These joints are often secured with wood glue and screws.

(left) "Getting the spite out" is the traditional term for the technique of softening and flexing a thin, pliable branch so it is easier to bend and shape in projects that require branches that curve or bend in large sweeps. Flexing the branch back and forth helps soften and tenderize the wood fibers so they bend easily, and makes it less likely you'll break the branch when attaching it to your project.

❧ Drilling pilot holes ensures that wood will not split. It also makes it easier to put in either a nail or a screw. If you are using green wood for decorating, you can get away without pilot holes if you are doing it 1½ inches or more from the end of the wood.

❧ When I want a tighter fit, I do what I call "sculpting." I create a hollow on the first piece of wood, so the second piece will fit snugly into it. I use an angle grinder which quickly carves the space I need, so I can join the two pieces.

❧ It is easiest to use this sculpting technique working from the front of a piece, but if you do, the nail or screw head will show. Sometimes this is fine, but for a fancier piece, I try to work from the back or the inside of a piece, so the nails and screws do not show. It is fussier work, but gives a higher quality appearance.

Gathering Materials

Be on the lookout for unusual, eccentric pieces of wood. These pieces were used to create the single chair shown on page 9.

The branches, vines, and small trees you'll need to build the projects in this book are quite easy to come by and usually are free for the asking. If you live in a rural area, any woods or brush thicket where you have permission to cut green wood will provide all the materials you need. But even if you live in the city, suitable branches are easy to come by. Neighbors pruning trees or hedges likely will be happy to have you cart away materials they will have to dispose of anyway. Each thunderstorm may deliver a harvest of furniture building materials in the form of branches dropped by the wind.

Park maintenance people can be an especially good source of materials. They may even appreciate some help with their work. Many towns will have a yard waste depot at their dump.

Remember that rustic projects can be built from just about any material, not just green wood. Sometimes demolition projects, scrap piles and dumps are good sources of usable pieces of wood. Old turned posts and railings can become chair or table legs; old siding or fence slats can become bench seats. I rescued some beautiful old boards from the back of a pickup truck on their way to the dump. They had come off an old shed and were 16-18" wide. You rarely see boards, or trees, of this width anymore.

And while this book mainly focuses on the use of wood, who is to say that rustic furniture has to be made of wood? Pay attention to any found objects you come across. One year, staying in Grand Manon in New Brunswick, I made a basket woven with seaweed. Another year,

along the beach I found an old plastic jug, lots of plastic rope in many colors, and bits of fish net, crab shells and sea shells to weave into a basket. I have experimented with old lobster traps. Deer antlers are nice materials. I love to put birds' nests on my work—now they are an amazing work of art. I love turned posts, and often old pieces of "regular" furniture can be incorporated into new pieces of rustic furniture. Whatever you can find that appeals to you can be fitted in somehow with your work.

Collecting grapevine is one of my least favorite jobs, but it is necessary because the material is interesting to use. No particular trick here, just perseverance.

I follow just a few rules in my collecting. I ask for permission from property owners to harvest materials. Most people are quite fine about that, as I take so little and what I do take is of little or no value to them. Often, they're quite pleased that I'm offering to clear away brush. I also try to remember to give thanks for what I am taking. Who do I thank? Mostly, I think, it is to the willow or dogwood or cedar itself that provides me with such enjoyment and is the source of my livelihood. And I am grateful for the woods and fields around me, to the atmosphere of these places that nourishes my spirit as I work. And I give thanks for the good fortune that allows me to spend my days like this, in beauty, working with nature.

I hope that you, too, are soothed by the beauty of the pieces you work with and the places in which you find them. I hope you have a wonderful time with these projects, and that they give you the basic skills to take off on your own and express yourself in your own way.

❧ Gather together a supply of pieces before you start, and sort them by shape and size. This is much easier than trying to harvest individual pieces as you need them for a project. This is the corner outside my workshop where I store straight pieces of varying sizes.

Hanging Shelf

This hanging shelf is a great project because it can be made in any size that fits the purpose you have in mind. Using these instructions, you can make any-thing from a small shelf to display collectibles to a sturdy shelf to hold books or kitchen supplies.

The project starts with a board for the shelf itself. I often use scraps leftover from pre-vious projects. You also need two branches for the uprights, two for the braces, and one for the top piece. It doesn't really matter what size the board and branches are, as long as the scale of each works with the others. A hanging shelf looks best when decorated with grapevine or small twigs. Use your imagination and whatever materials you have on hand.

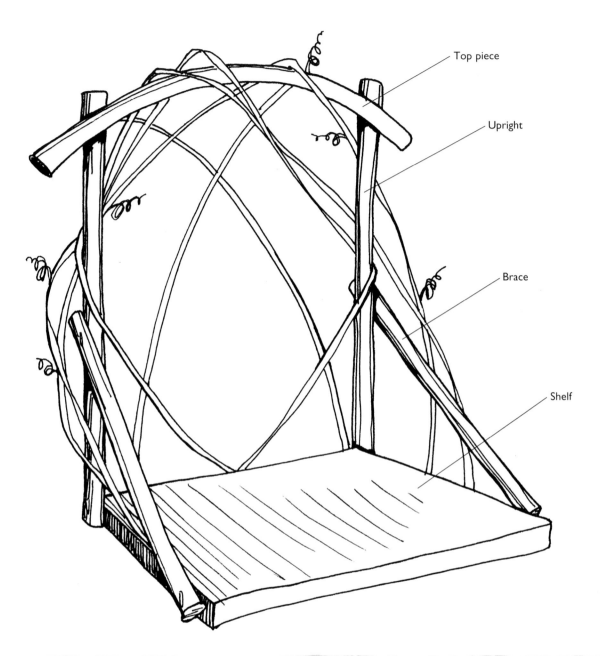

Top piece

Upright

Brace

Shelf

Tools:

- Power drill
- Staple gun
- Pruning saw or sharp pruning shears

Materials:

- (1) Shelf: a board 4" to 8" wide, and 12" to 18" long
- (2) Uprights: cedar branches, 16" long
- (2) Braces: cedar branches about 6" long
- (1) Top piece: an interesting branch about 20" long
- Grapevines or twigs
- Assorted screws, nails and staples

Step 1: Lay the shelf board on its long edge. Position one of the 16-inch uprights perpendicular to the shelf, near the end. Drill a pilot hole and fasten the upright to the shelf with a 1½- to 2-inch screw.

Step 2: Drill a pilot hole at each end of the 6-inch braces. Make sure that the upright is still perpendicular to the base board, then position a brace diagonally from the corner of the shelf to the upright, and fasten with screws.

Step 3: Add the other 16-inch upright and 6-inch brace to the opposite end of the shelf board.

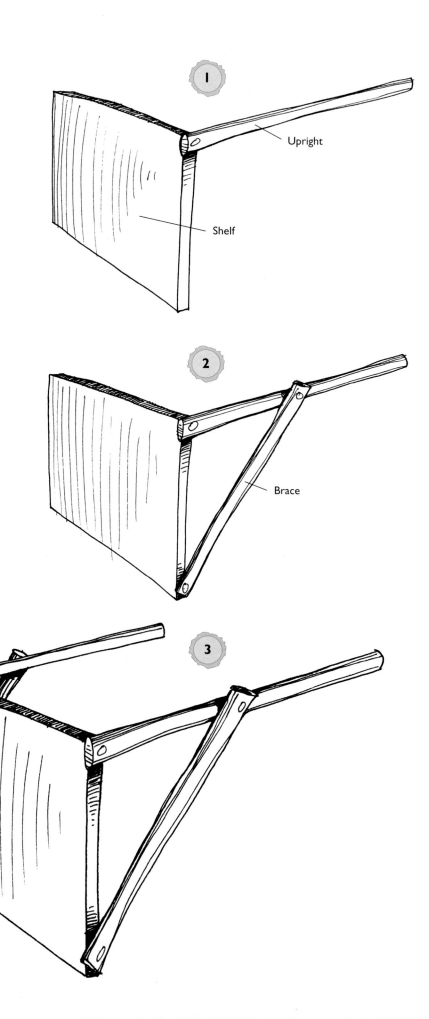

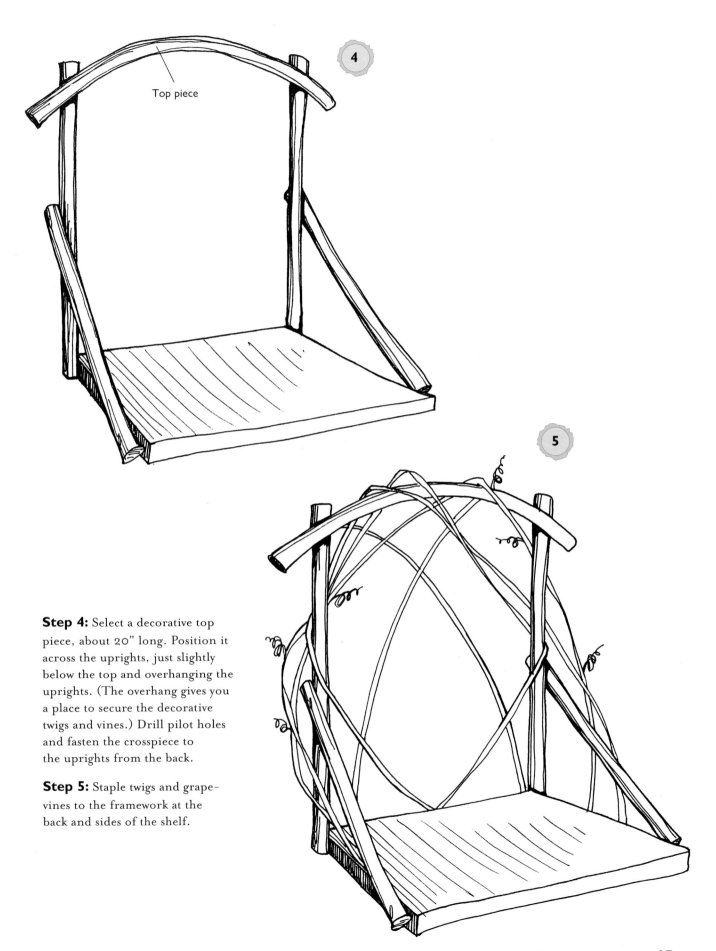

Top piece

④

⑤

Step 4: Select a decorative top piece, about 20" long. Position it across the uprights, just slightly below the top and overhanging the uprights. (The overhang gives you a place to secure the decorative twigs and vines.) Drill pilot holes and fasten the crosspiece to the uprights from the back.

Step 5: Staple twigs and grape-vines to the framework at the back and sides of the shelf.

Pot Trellis

Container gardens are so popular because they're easy to grow and maintain, but they can be a little boring if everything is the same height. When you add a trellis to a pot or other container, you add height to the display. It can also be planted in the ground as a garden accent among growing plants (as shown).

These rustic pot trellises are ideal for climbing vines of all sorts. A large trellis could support ivy, morning glories, or honeysuckle. A slightly smaller version would be an ideal companion for sweet peas.

One thought about shape and scale before we start: This trellis is designed to fan out to the sides. To create this shape, you need a range of curved sticks, some more curved than others. Try to arrange the sticks in a basic fan shape, but don't worry too much about making it perfect. The beauty of these projects lies in their unique character.

Tools:

- ∾ Pruning saw or sharp pruning shears
- ∾ Sharp knife, such as a sturdy pocket knife
- ∾ Power drill

Materials:

- ∾ Assorted screws
- ∾ (1) Center post: straight branch ½" to ¾" in diameter, of chosen length (ours is about 30")
- ∾ (2) Inner slats: gently curved branches, 4" to 6" shorter than center post
- ∾ (2) Outer slats: severely curved branches, 4" to 6" shorter than center post
- ∾ (1) Bottom brace: straight branch, about 6" long
- ∾ (2) Arches: curved branches, (ours are about 24" long)

Step 1: Select a straight stick as a center post, then whittle it to a point at one end. Lay one of the inner slats on each side of the center post, starting 6" to 8" above the pointed end. Put one of the outer slats on each side of the inner slats. (The curves of each stick should point away from the center stick.)

1

Inner slats

Outer slats

Center post

Arches

2

Bottom brace

Step 2: Cut a bottom brace and position it across the base of the trellis body, 4" to 5" above the ends of the slats. Drill pilot holes and screw the brace in place. Lay the arches across the fan of the trellis, a few inches down from the top. Drill pilot holes and screw these in place, too.

Cedar Carrier

This carrier is designed to hold six 5- to 6-inch flower pots, but I find I more commonly use it to carry my tools. It could also be used as a decorative planter set on a tabletop.

If your rough-cut cedar boards are warped at all, try to arrange them so the carrier doesn't wobble.

An interesting variation of this project is shown sitting on the window ledge in the photo on page 12.

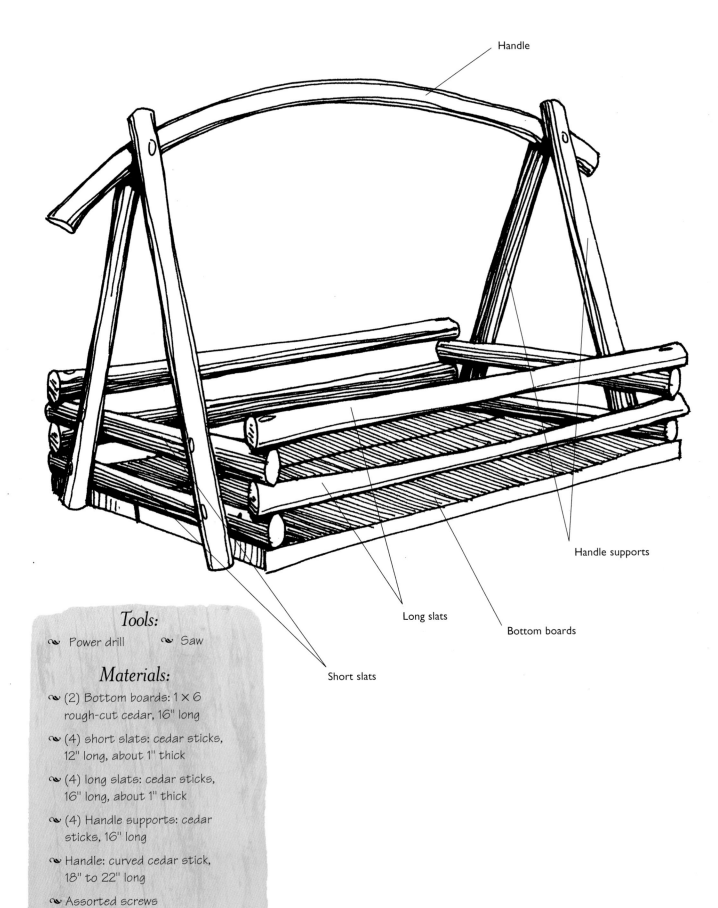

Handle

Handle supports

Long slats

Bottom boards

Short slats

Tools:

- Power drill   - Saw

Materials:

- (2) Bottom boards: 1 × 6 rough-cut cedar, 16" long

- (4) short slats: cedar sticks, 12" long, about 1" thick

- (4) long slats: cedar sticks, 16" long, about 1" thick

- (4) Handle supports: cedar sticks, 16" long

- Handle: curved cedar stick, 18" to 22" long

- Assorted screws

Step 1: Put the two 16" bottom boards beside one another on the work surface with their long sides together. Place a 12" short slat across the ends of the boards and drill four evenly-spaced pilot holes along each stick. Attach each slat to the bottom boards with four screws. Two screws in the end of each board prevent the boards from warping.

Short slats

Bottom boards

1

Step 2: Lay a 16" long slat across the front and back, on top of the short slats. Overlap the ends like logs stacked for a log cabin. Drill pilot holes, placing them carefully so that the screws won't hit the ones on the slats below. Put one screw in at each corner. Continue in this way until you have two rows of each size.

2

Long slats

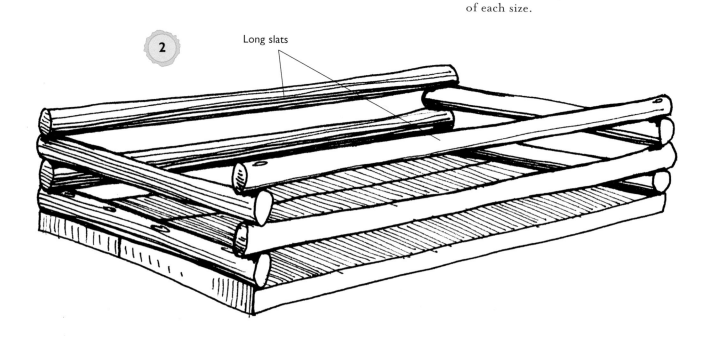

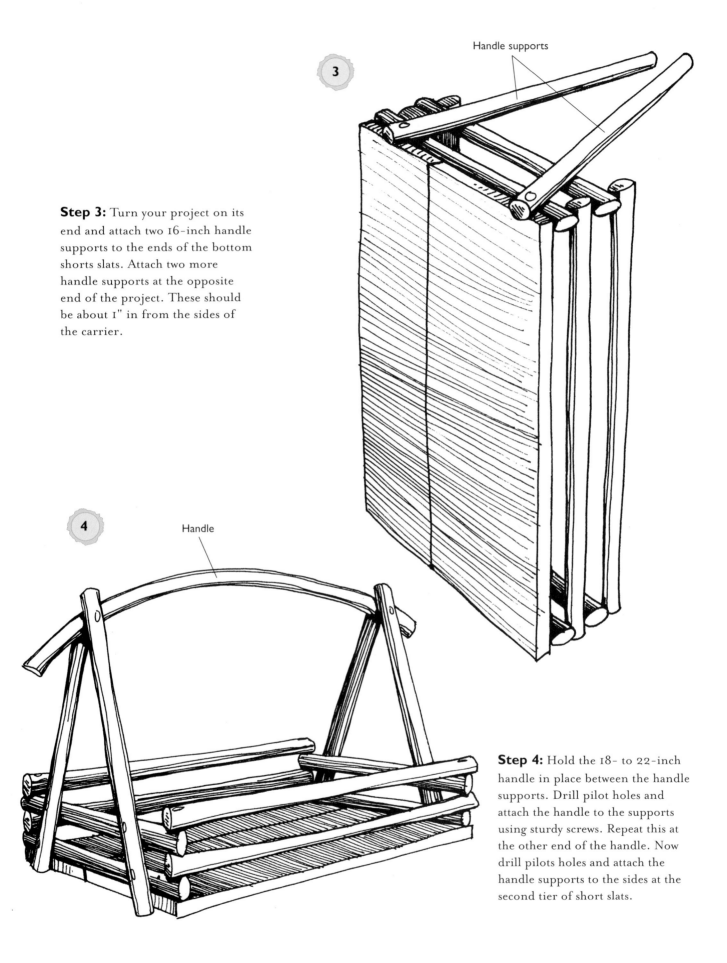

Handle supports

3

Step 3: Turn your project on its end and attach two 16-inch handle supports to the ends of the bottom shorts slats. Attach two more handle supports at the opposite end of the project. These should be about 1" in from the sides of the carrier.

4

Handle

Step 4: Hold the 18- to 22-inch handle in place between the handle supports. Drill pilot holes and attach the handle to the supports using sturdy screws. Repeat this at the other end of the handle. Now drill pilots holes and attach the handle supports to the sides at the second tier of short slats.

Stars

Stars are a fun and easy project, which can be made any size, if you use lighter stock for small stars and heavier stock for big ones. I find this is a good way to use long, thin pieces of wood that are too uneven for other projects. The stars may even look better for the twists, bumps and curves when you use stock with this kind of character.

Once you have mastered the technique, stars are quick and easy to make, as well as satisfying.

Five-pointed stars look good on top of an obelisk, decorated with lights as a Christmas tree, or hung on a wall by themselves.

Tools:
- ∞ Pruning shears or pruning saw
- ∞ Power drill

Materials:
- ∞ (5) Thin branches of equal length
- ∞ Vines for decoration
- ∞ Small screws

Five-pointed Star

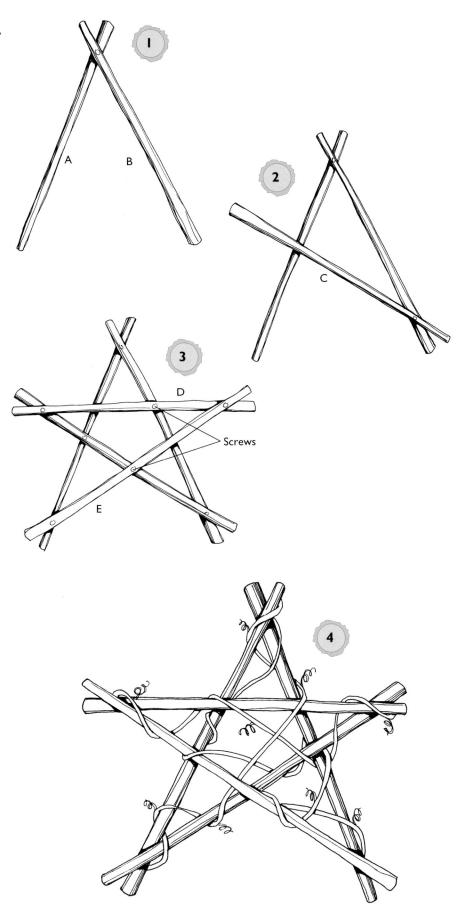

Step 1: Take five sticks of equal length. I would suggest that you start with a fairly large star, because small things are often more challenging to make than large ones (18 inches is a nice size that I use a lot). Lay the first stick (A) at an angle. Lay the second stick (B) onto the first stick, creating sort of a V at the top. This V provides a place to secure the vines when they are wrapped around the star. It also makes it possible to screw the pieces together without necessarily drilling pilot holes. Screw the two pieces together.

Step 2: Place your third stick (C) onto the second in a similar fashion. Fasten this in place.

Step 3: Continue in this way until you have all five sticks fastened together. Screw the last stick into the free end of the first stick. Because the whole thing moves about, adjust them to form a well-balanced star. Put one or two screws in at the center joints. If the pieces don't lie flat, don't worry, as this will not be noticeable on the finished product.

Step 4: Use fairly fine grapevine to decorate the star. Wind the vine in whatever way looks pleasing to you. Decorate the side where no screws show.

Six-pointed Star

Take six sticks of the same length. You are going to create two triangles, and then put one on top of the other to create the effect of a star with six points.

Step 1: Place the first stick on the table. Take your second stick and place it on the first stick, a short distance from the end, creating a V as shown in the drawing. Fasten with one screw.

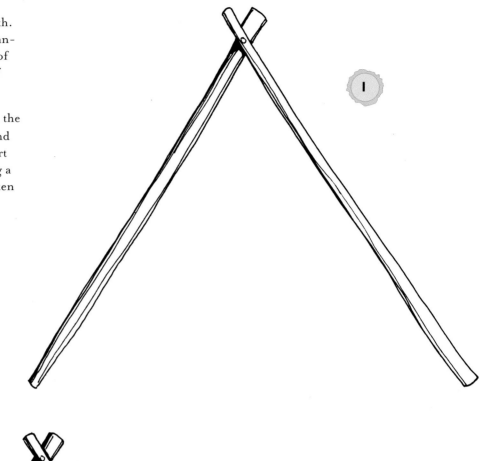

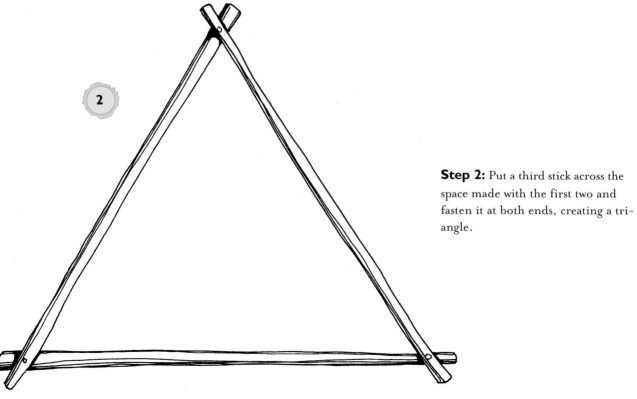

Step 2: Put a third stick across the space made with the first two and fasten it at both ends, creating a triangle.

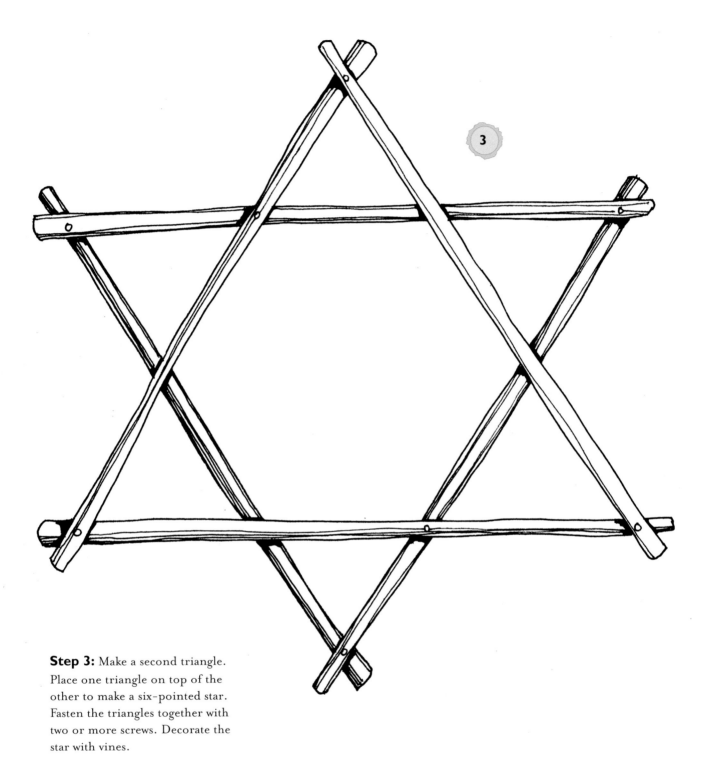

Step 3: Make a second triangle. Place one triangle on top of the other to make a six-pointed star. Fasten the triangles together with two or more screws. Decorate the star with vines.

Hanging Rack

This rack was designed by a client for drying the plastic bags she washes for recycling. They are also handy for drying herbs and flowers, hanging mitts and hats, or hanging your pruning shears and other gardening implements. You can make this any size you want, using heavy or light pieces of wood, and adding any number of hooks.

For this piece, you need four branches or small tree trunks that fork out in such a way that you have an upright and a branch sticking out at a bit of an upward angle for the hooks. The best way to go about this is to find the four main pieces, cut them to the same length, and then cut the pieces to fit across the top and bottom. We staggered the "hooks," which leaves plenty of room for things to hang, but you may prefer to line them up at the same height. Many of these decisions depend on the characteristics of the branches you choose.

Tools:

- Pruning saw or sharp shears
- Power drill
- Hammer
- Staple gun

Materials:

- (4) Uprights: branches with forks as "hooks," 12" to 18" long
- (2) Crosspieces: straight branches 24" to 36" long
- Vines or decorative branches
- Screws of suitable length, depending on thickness of branches

Step 1: Position the four uprights with the "hooks" facing forward and pointing up. When you see how long the rack will be, trim the two straight crosspieces to fit across the top and bottom of the project. Drill pilot holes and put a small screw at each joint between a branch and the top and bottom of the rack.

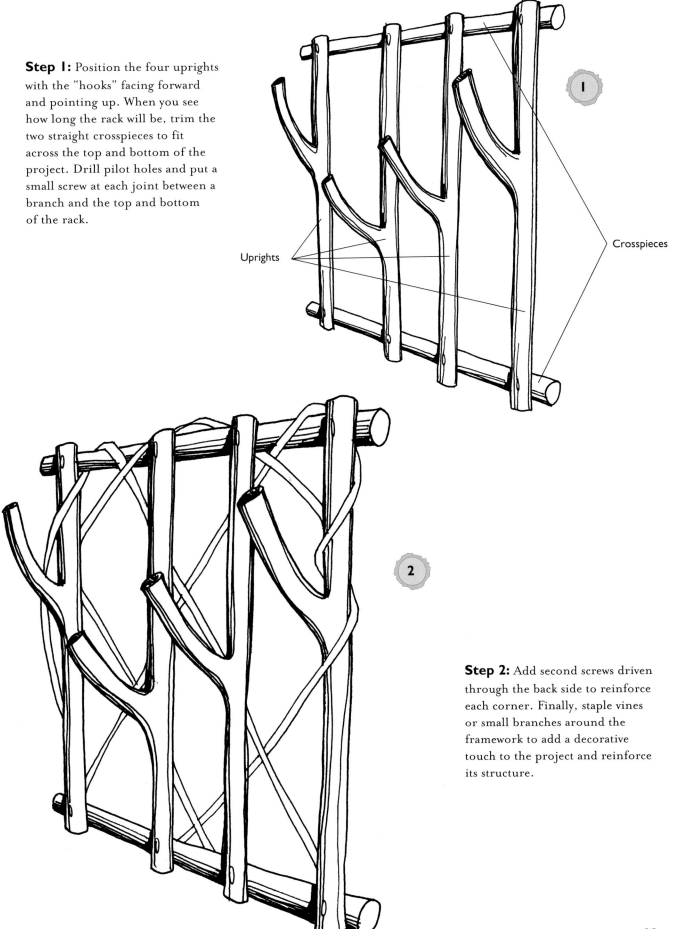

Uprights

Crosspieces

1

2

Step 2: Add second screws driven through the back side to reinforce each corner. Finally, staple vines or small branches around the framework to add a decorative touch to the project and reinforce its structure.

Tripod Planter

While this tripod was designed to hold a flowerpot, one student of mine uses it for her salad bowl so the bowl doesn't take up space on the dinner table. She also puts a pumpkin in it for Halloween. Once you get your imagination running, you'll find all sorts of uses for a tripod like this.

This project is a good way to use branches that may be too twisted or oddly shaped for other purposes. Remember that if you use this project where it will be out in the weather, the vine may need to be replaced after a year or two.

Step 1: Cut three sturdy legs to equal lengths, somewhat longer than the planned height of your planter. (I usually cut them at about 32 inches.) This next part is a bit tricky: Hold the poles in your non-dominant hand (your left hand if you're right-handed; right hand if you're left-handed), about 8" down from the top. Spread the poles out so the bottoms are equal distances from one another and the tops form a space into which you could place a flowerpot. (We will be enclosing this space, so you have to use your imagination here.) Drill pilot holes and attach each pole to the one on each side of it, using heavy screws. Grip one pole in each hand and see if they move at all. If they do, add another screw or two at different angles. The tripod needs to be solid.

Step 2: Wrap a flexible vine around the top of the tripod to create a bowl shape for a flowerpot to sit in. Use small nails or staples to secure the vine as you proceed. (I like to weave the vine in and out of itself, which produces an interesting texture.)

Tools:

- Hand saw
- Hammer
- Power drill
- Staple gun
- Pruning shears

Materials:

- (3) Legs: sturdy poles, 1" to 1½" in diameter, 32" to 36" long
- Small vines
- Sturdy screws long enough to join the poles
- Small nails or staples to attach the vines

Planter Easel

Don't let the number of steps in the instructions scare you, even if you don't have a lot of experience yet. This project is divided into quite a number of steps (especially if you're building the picture frame instead of using an old one), but they're all fairly simple and easy to do.

When you finish building the easel, line the box with plastic and gravel and fill it with plants. The plants will look as though they are a framed picture. (Geraniums, lobelia, or wave petunias look lovely.) If you want to train a vine up the posts, you can plant it in either the box or in the ground beneath the easel.

Tools:
~ Power drill   ~ Circular saw

Materials:

~ (3) Legs: straight poles, 1" to 1½" in diameter, 6 feet long

~ (1) Long brace: 32" long

~ (2) Short braces: straight sticks, 16" long

~ 7 ft. of cedar 1 × 4s or 1 × 5s

~ An old picture frame or four pieces of 1 × 4 cedar lumber, 28 to 30 inches

~ Nails and screws of the appropriate lengths

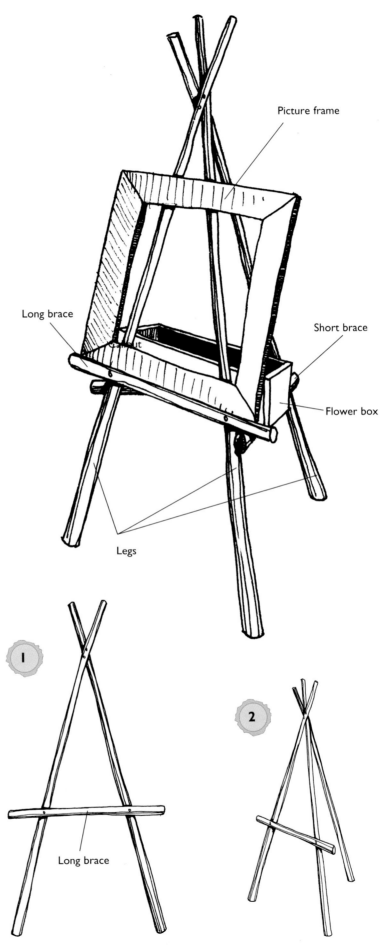

Picture frame

Long brace

Short brace

Flower box

Legs

Step 1: Take two of the 7-foot legs and line up the thick ends with the edge of a worktable. The tops should cross, leaving a space at the top for the third piece to fit into later. Drill two pilot holes and screw the poles together at the top. Next, take the 32-inch long brace and place it across the first two legs, about 36 inches from the bottom and centered across the legs. Drill pilot holes and drive a screw into each joint.

Step 2: Stand the structure up, and lean the third 7-foot leg into it at the top. Drill pilot holes and put in two screws to connect the third leg to each of the first two.

Long brace

Step 3: Run a 16-inch short brace from one front leg to the back, just below the 32-inch long brace, and parallel to the ground. Drill pilot holes and fasten the short brace in place with a screw at each joint. Repeat this process to add the second short brace, which completes the stand.

Step 4: Cut three 25" cedar boards. Set one of the boards flat on the work surface and another perpendicular to it. Secure the joint with three evenly spaced nails or screws. Repeat to add the other side to the box.

Step 5: Measure the openings at the ends of the box; cut two pieces of cedar lumber to fit. Attach the ends to the box, driving nails or screws along each side and across the bottoms. Drill a few drainage holes in the floor of the box.

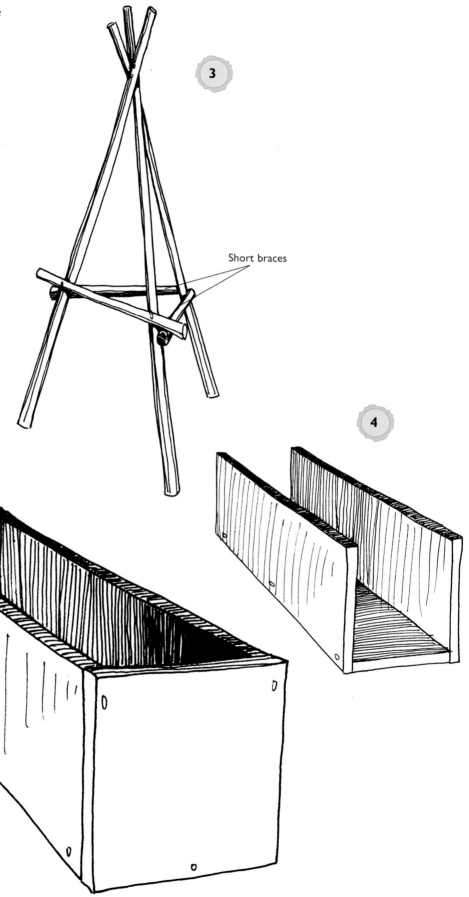

Short braces

Step 6: If you're making the picture frame, cut each end of the 27-inch cedar 1 × 4s at a 45° angle. Lay the boards together in a square. At each corner, drive a screw in at an angle to join the two pieces. Then, close to the inside corner, drive a screw from the back of one piece, across the joint, and into the other. Add another screw going the opposite direction, about halfway along the joint. This can be tricky. Make sure you have not attached the frame to the table. Drive the final screw from the outside edge of one piece, through the joint and into the other.

Step 7: Place the picture frame, face forward, onto the long brace of the easel. Drill pilot holes and drive screws in from the back in three places where the frame touches the poles. Put the box through the legs and rest it on the supports there. Attach the box to the supports with two screws on each side.

Planter Chair

You can use this chair to hold plants in containers, or you can put the plants directly in the chair. If you line it with plastic, the boards will last longer, but you will have to provide some drainage for the water. You could put holes in the plastic or a layer of gravel on the bottom before you add your soil. I have done a Poppa Bear, Mamma Bear, Baby Bear version of this, which makes an interesting grouping.

I got the idea for this design while passing through a lovely small Virginia town called Sperryville. There was a gardening shop there with many unusual rustic pieces. Sperryville—and the garden center there—is worth visiting, if you have a chance.

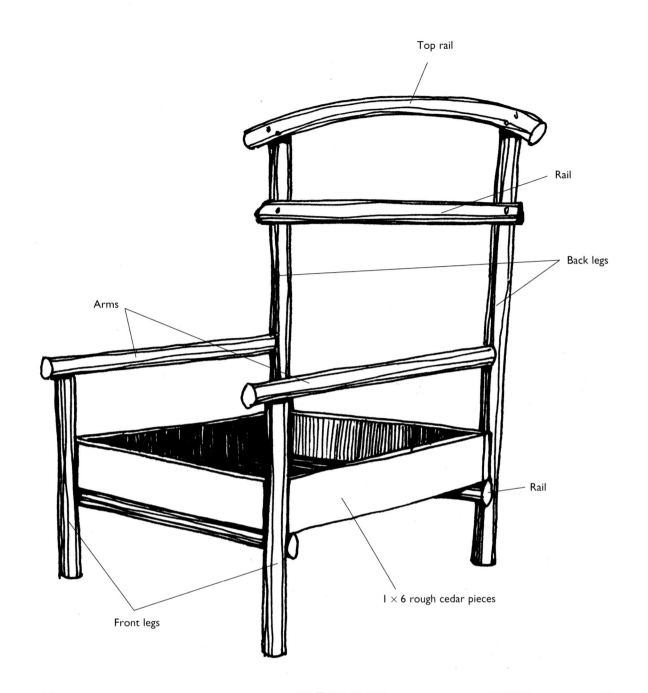

Top rail

Rail

Back legs

Arms

Front legs

Rail

1 × 6 rough cedar pieces

Tools:

 ∾ Power drill   ∾ Circular saw

Materials:

 ∾ (2) Back legs: 1½" to 2" in diameter, 30" long

 ∾ (2) Front legs: 1½" to 2" in diameter, 24" long

 ∾ (2) Arms: 1½" to 2" in diameter, cut to desired length

 ∾ (3) Rails: 1½" to 2" in diameter, 20" long

 ∾ (1) Top rail: slightly curved, 1" to 2" in diameter, about 24" long

 ∾ An 8-ft. rough-cut cedar 1 × 6 or a collection of scraps, each at least 12" long

 ∾ Screws in assorted lengths

Step 1: Position two 30-inch back legs about 16" apart, and position a curved top rail across the top. Cut two 20" rails to fit across the back; place the first rail 10" from the bottom of the legs and the second about 8" from the top. Drill two pilot holes at each juncture, but drive a screw in only one of the holes. Adjust the shape, and then add a second screw at each juncture.

Step 2: To construct a front frame, position two 24" legs and cut a 20" rail to fit between them, 10" from the bottom. (The rails form a shelf to support the planter box.)

Step 3: Lay two 12-inch 1 × 6s on the table and cut 1 × 6s to fit across the ends. Drill pilot holes and attach each side with four screws.

Step 4: Cut 1 × 6s to fit the sides of the box; drill pilot holes and attach the sides with two screws on each side.

Step 5: Prop up the back and front frames, and position the box between them. (Place the frames so the braces face one another.) Drill pilot holes and fasten the box firmly to the front and back frames. Cut branches for arms, and then drill pilot holes and attach them to the back and front frames.

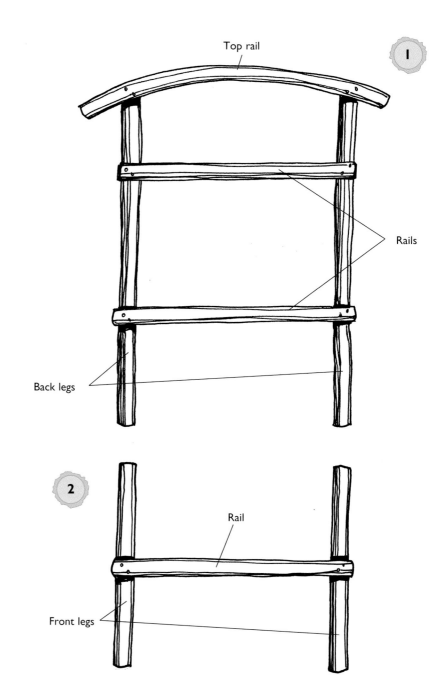

1

Top rail

Rails

Back legs

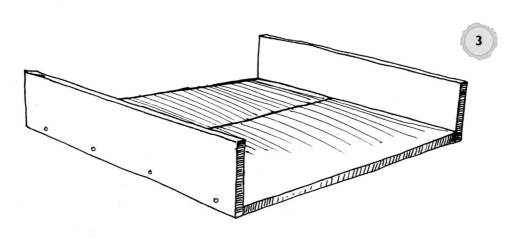

2

Rail

Front legs

3

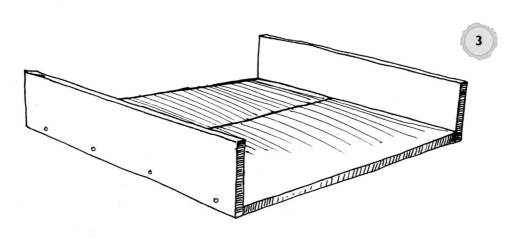

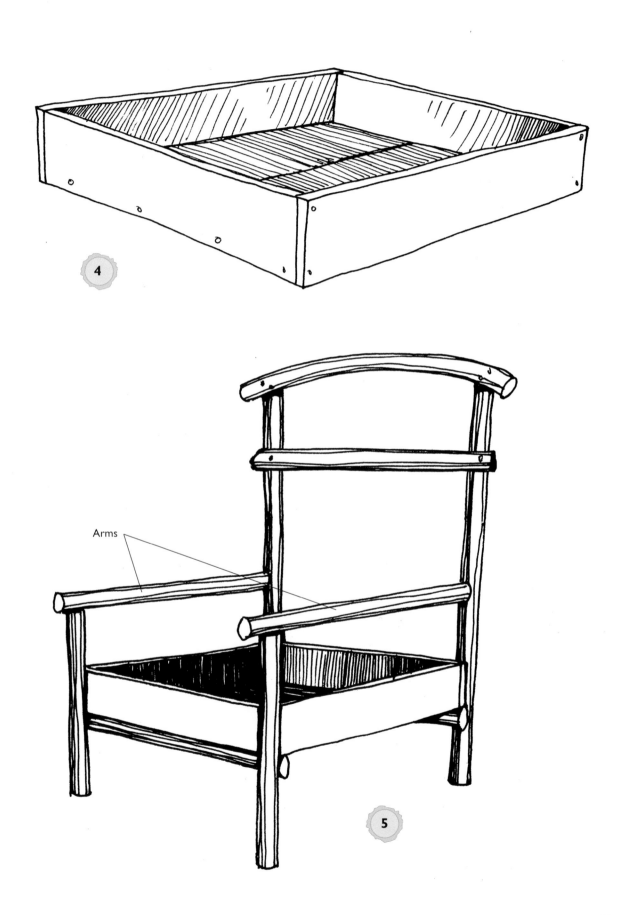

Arms

Frame Trellis

The base of this trellis needs to be straight; however, the top can be straight, arched, or any other shape you find interesting. It can be any size you want, so I've not listed specific measurements in the materials list. Unless it's going be fastened to a wall, the top doesn't need to lie flat, so this trellis may be an opportunity to use an unusual piece that isn't suitable for other projects.

This trellis can be built like the gate (page 76), although because of its size, it needs quite a bit more support built into it. The frame can be decorated with branches and vines, but don't use small branches if you'll be removing dead vines in the fall. Remember to include diagonals in your design to provide bracing and prevent "racking," or loss of shape. Secure the diagonals to the framework and to each other. The diagonal bracing can be provided by small angled branches that fork off from the vertical posts, as you see in this photo. In the project directions, though, I'll show you how to add these supports after the vertical posts are installed.

If you use vines for decoration, or branches from a softwood tree, remember that they may need to be replaced after a few years. Cedar and hardwood branches tend to last longer than softer woods. Also, the thicker the branches are, the longer they will last.

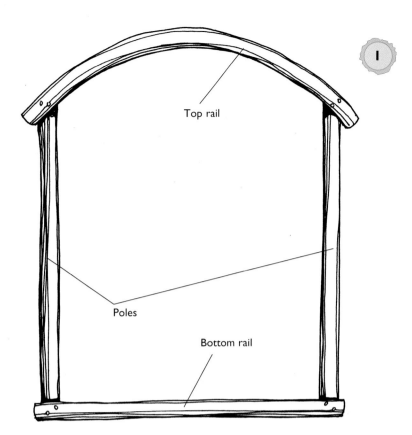

Top rail

Poles

Bottom rail

Tools:

- Power drill
- Hammer, shears, and staple gun (optional)

Materials:

- (4 or 5) Poles: straight branches of chosen length
- (1) Bottom rail: straight branch of chosen length
- (1) Top rail: curved branch
- Vines or branches (optional)
- Assorted screws, nails, and staples

Step 1: Lay the poles and the top and bottom rails on the ground or a large table, and drill two pilot holes as far apart as possible at each joint. Drive one screw into each joint. Make sure the sides are perpendicular to the base and put in the second screws. (If you're ready for more advanced designs, you may not want the sides to be perpendicular, but we're starting with a simple design here.)

Step 2: If the trellis is a small- to medium-sized one, go ahead and decorate it now. If it's large, add two or three braces between the top and bottom rails. As you add decorations, arrange the branches to create diagonals and triangular bracing. Drive screws to attach the branches to one another as well as to the frame and braces.

Fan Trellis

This trellis is not quite as easy as it looks. The biggest challenge is finding branches with just the right curves. While they can be bent a bit and held where you want with screws, it's important not to put too much stress on your trellis or it will twist and bend out of shape. Eastern white cedar is great because its branches grow in long, graceful curves, such as the ones you need for this project.

While this is a fairly classic design, it lends itself to many variations. You may want to play around with it and see what you can add to the basic design.

Step 1: Start with the long, thin piece of wood that will be your center post. (It's more likely to be a small tree trunk than a branch.) Lay this piece on your worksurface. Find two slightly curved slats similar in dimension to the center post. Lay one of them on each side of the center post, with the curves fanning away from the center. Now find two sharply curved slats and place one of them on each outside edge. Again, the curves should fan away from the center.

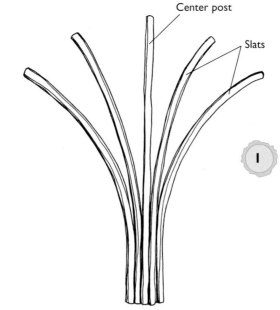

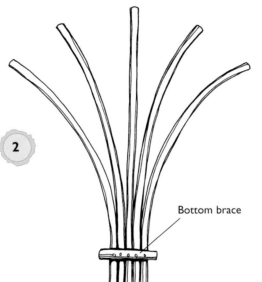

Step 2: Now you need a short bottom brace similar in thickness to the base of the pieces already in place. It needs to be long enough to span the base of the trellis with a bit hanging over on each side. Put this brace across the base of the fan, a nice distance up from the bottom. Drill pilot holes and screw the brace into place. Make sure your screws are long enough to go deeply into the fan pieces, as this is a place where they tend to pull apart.

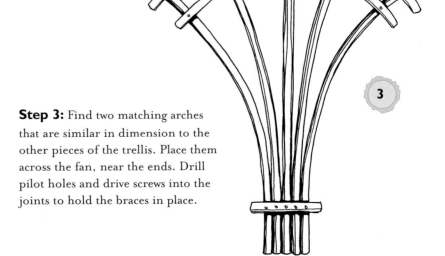

Tools:
- Power drill
- Pruning shears
- Pruning saw

Materials:
- (1) Center post: straight branch of chosen length about 1" in diameter at base
- (4) Slats: curved posts, equal in size to center post
- (2) Arches: curved branches of chosen length
- (1) Bottom brace: straight stick, chosen to fit
- Assorted screws

Step 3: Find two matching arches that are similar in dimension to the other pieces of the trellis. Place them across the fan, near the ends. Drill pilot holes and drive screws into the joints to hold the braces in place.

Ladder Trellis

This project is designed to lean against a wall or fence. Besides being a great support for plants, a ladder trellis can break up the monotony of a large, blank wall, or provide a decorative focus between a pair of windows.

A trellis can be attached directly to the wall or leaned against it. If you attach it to a building, put spacers behind the branches so they don't sit directly on the siding. Make spacers by attaching small pieces of plastic or copper plumbing tubing to the trellis.

If you lean the trellis against a wall, anchor it well. You can drive wooden stakes, iron rebar, or steel T-bar (used as posts for wire fencing) into the ground beside the ladder poles and attach the poles to them. Secure wooden stakes to the trellis with long screws; wrap wire tightly around the poles and the rebar or T-bar.

Tools:

- Power drill
- Pruning saw
- Pruning shears (optional)

Materials:

- (2) Posts: sturdy poles, 6 ft. long
- (6) Rungs: 14" branches, equal in diameter to posts
- Screws of appropriate lengths
- Vines (optional)

Step 1: Lay the posts side by side with the bottoms even. Mark them at one-foot intervals, starting at the base. Cut six 14-inch rungs. (The rungs can be similar in size to your poles or slightly smaller.)

Step 2: Place the rungs between the poles at the marks. Drill pilot holes through the sides of the poles and into the rungs. Attach the rungs with long, strong screws. (If the ladder doesn't feel solid, add some bracing.) Decorate the poles and rungs with twigs or vines.

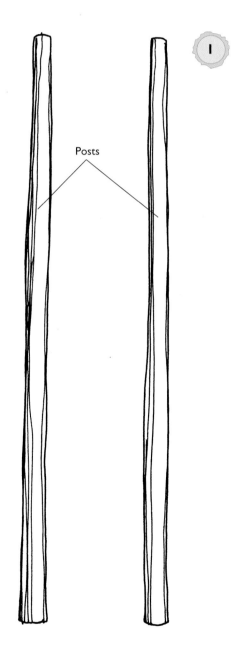

Posts

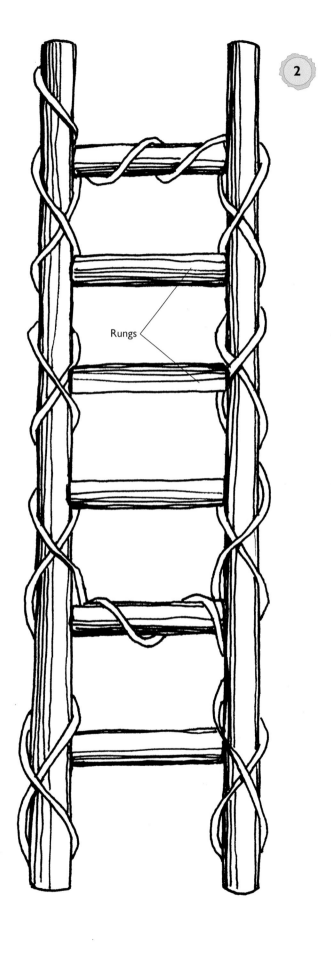

Rungs

Vegetable Trellis

We grow heritage tomatoes on this trellis, because they grow 8 or 9 feet tall, and use a shorter version for pickling cucumbers. We build our trellises so that they can be easily moved, because we rotate the use of our planting beds and like to store the trellises over the winter.

When planning a trellis, match its size to its purpose and to the vegetables you'll be growing. Many trellises are built too small for their intended use. Perennial vines continue to grow almost indefinitely, and even annuals grow 10 to 20 feet in a summer.

Tools:

- ❧ Power drill
- ❧ Hand saw

Materials:

- ❧ (6) Legs: straight poles of desired height (we used 7-ft. legs)
- ❧ (6) Rails: straight poles of equal length
- ❧ (10) Braces: straight poles of various lengths
- ❧ Assorted screws

Step 1: Take two long legs and lay them on your worksurface so that they make a V at the top. (This V will be the support for one of your crosspieces.) At the place where they cross, drill two pilot holes spaced as far apart as possible. Drive deck screws or strong nails into the pilot holes to join the pieces.

Step 2: Starting at the base, mark both poles at 1-foot intervals. Now cut the braces that will span the distance between the two poles, creating an A-frame ladder effect. Drill pilot holes and drive screws into the joints to hold the braces in place.

Step 3: Stand the piece up and add a third leg to create a tripod. The top of this pole needs to sit to one side of the other two so it doesn't fill the space at the top. (The top crosspiece will fit in that space.) Repeat steps 1 through 3 to make a second tripod.

Step 4: Place rails between the tripods. Attach each rail to the braces. (The length of these poles will be determined by how you plan to use the trellis.) Keep in mind that the poles will sag if they span too great a distance. Choose stout poles or add a brace in the middle of the span.

Legs

Braces

Leg

Rails

Planter

This small decorative planter can be built in a very short amount of time and makes a perfect accent to a deck or patio. Many people build a lot of these planters, scattering them about the garden as a unifying accent. And they can be moved around at will, letting you redecorate whenever you want.

Because of the narrow footprint, you may have trouble with the planter wobbling, especially if it's placed on a hard-surface patio. If necessary, you can shear the bottoms of the legs until the planter rests solidly.

Tools:

- Power drill
- Pruning shears
- Hammer
- Staple gun
- Saw

Materials:

- (4) Legs: 36" branches
- (4) 10" rails
- (4) 12" rails
- (2) 14" rails
- (4 to 7) Shelf slats: cut to fit
- Decorative branches
- Assorted nails, screws, and staples

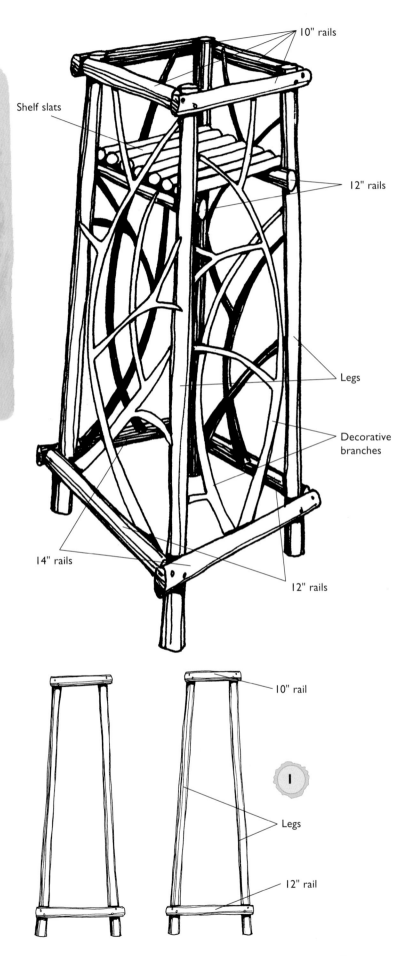

10" rails

Shelf slats

12" rails

Legs

Decorative branches

14" rails

12" rails

10" rail

Legs

12" rail

Step 1: Put two 36-inch legs on a worktable; line up the ends with the edge of the table. Place a 10-inch top rail across the top, flush with the top of the legs. Drill two pilot holes at each juncture and drive a screw into one pilot hole at each. Place a 12-inch bottom rail about 4 inches from the ends of the poles; the brace should be parallel to the top piece and flush with the sides of the poles. Again, drill two pilot holes and drive one screw into each juncture. Now check to make sure the frame is lined up right (it's supposed to lean in a bit at the top). When you're satisfied, drive a second screw into each juncture. Repeat this process to make a second frame.

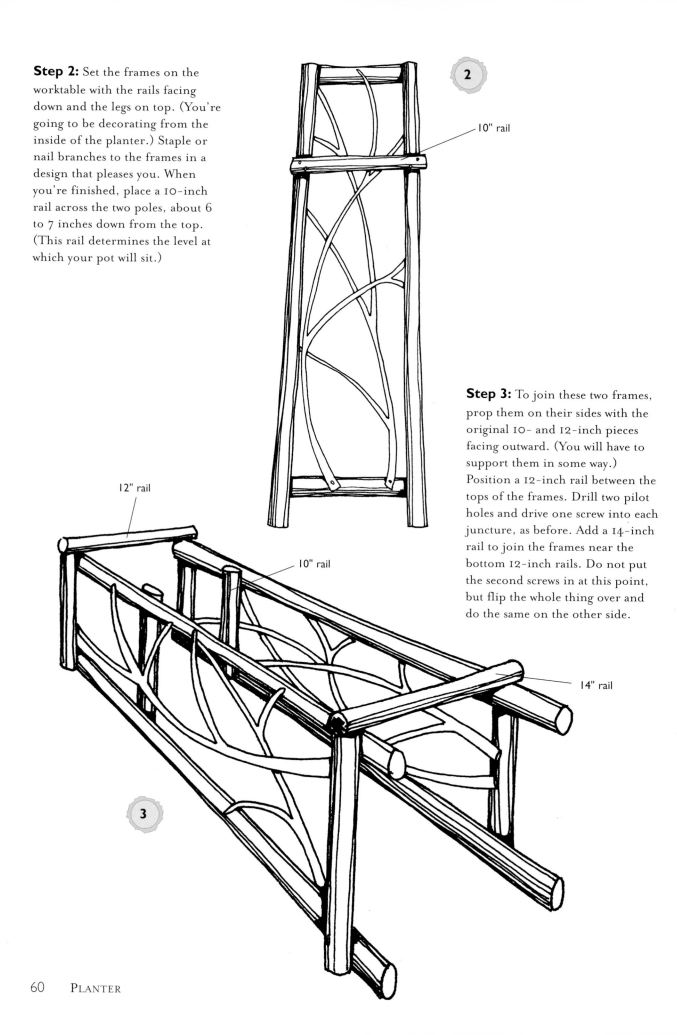

Step 2: Set the frames on the worktable with the rails facing down and the legs on top. (You're going to be decorating from the inside of the planter.) Staple or nail branches to the frames in a design that pleases you. When you're finished, place a 10-inch rail across the two poles, about 6 to 7 inches down from the top. (This rail determines the level at which your pot will sit.)

10" rail

Step 3: To join these two frames, prop them on their sides with the original 10- and 12-inch pieces facing outward. (You will have to support them in some way.) Position a 12-inch rail between the tops of the frames. Drill two pilot holes and drive one screw into each juncture, as before. Add a 14-inch rail to join the frames near the bottom 12-inch rails. Do not put the second screws in at this point, but flip the whole thing over and do the same on the other side.

12" rail

10" rail

14" rail

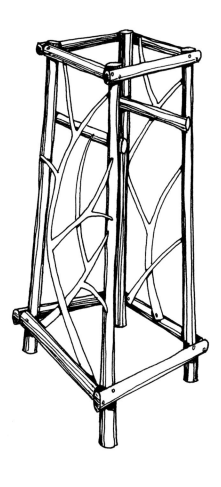

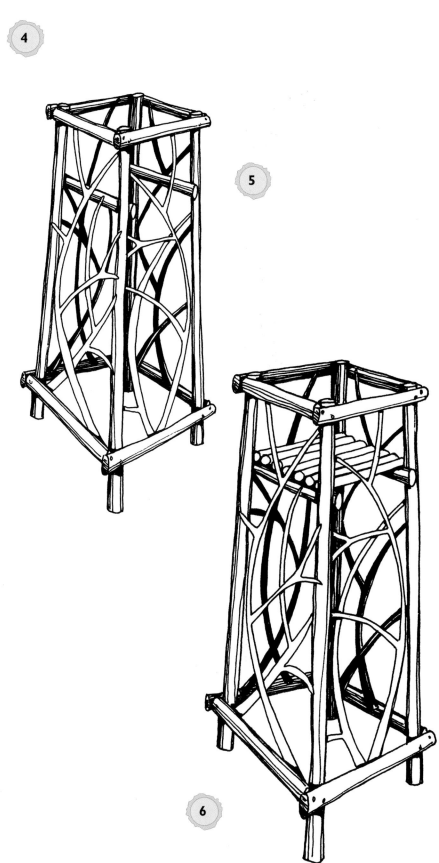

Step 4: Stand your frame up. It may be leaning to one side or the other, or otherwise be askew. Adjust the frame until it's even and all four legs touch the ground. (You may have to put pressure on from the top.) Once it's solid, put a second screw into each juncture on both sides of the planter.

Step 5: Decorate the two remaining sides from the inside. (This may be a bit awkward, but you can do it.)

Step 6: With your planter standing up, cut short branches to span the rails that are 6 to 7 inches down from the top. Position the branches, drill pilot holes, and fasten the branches at both ends.

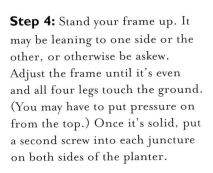

Obelisks

Obelisks look glorious in a
garden, rising grandly above other
garden structures. They're also
handy for supporting long vines
and tall plants. If you live in an
open area, obelisks can really
catch the wind. To anchor an
obelisk, pound a couple stakes
into the ground and wire them
to the centers of the crosspieces.

In the winter, decorate your
obelisk with fresh greens and
small lights for a festive touch
in the garden.

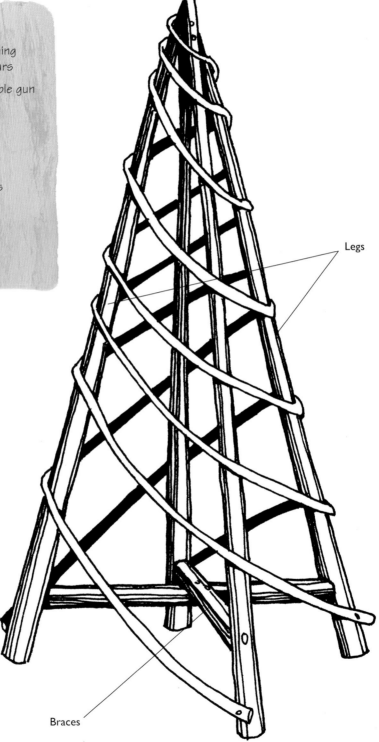

Tools:

- Power drill
- Hammer
- Saw
- Pruning shears
- Staple gun

Materials:

- (4) Legs: 7-ft. poles of similar thickness
- (2) Braces: 20" branches
- Branches or vines
- Assorted nails, screws, and staples

Legs

Braces

Step 1: Lay two of the 7-foot legs on the worktable with the bases aligned with the edge of the table and about 2 feet apart. Cross the tops of the poles, creating a slight "X." At the juncture, drill two pilot holes as far apart as possible and drive screws into them. Place a 20-inch brace between the two poles, parallel to the edge of the table. Drill pilot holes in from the side, through the first leg and into the center of the 20-inch brace; drive a strong screw into the joint. Fasten the other end of the brace to the second leg.

Step 2: Stand the frame upright. (You'll probably have to prop it against the worktable.) Place the base of the third leg about a foot away from the table edge, centered between the other two legs. Lay the top of the pole at the top of the frame. Drill pilot holes and fasten the third leg to the others.

Step 3: Move the frame away from the table and add the fourth leg as described in Step 2. Put the other 20-inch brace (which may need to be cut a bit shorter), between the third and fourth poles, resting on top of the original brace. Drill pilot holes and drive screws through the third and fourth legs and into this brace. Where the two braces meet, drill two pilot holes as far apart as possible and drive screws into the joint.

Step 4: Decorate the obelisk with branches or vines. I most commonly fasten cedar branches at angles going up the obelisk. Sometimes I mark the legs at one-foot intervals, wrap a thick grapevine in a spiral from the base to the top and then wrap another vine in a spiral from the other direction.

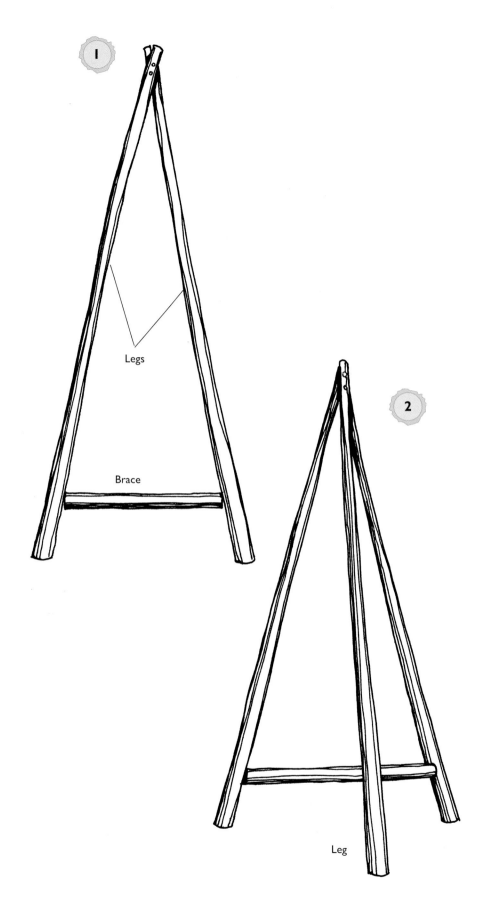

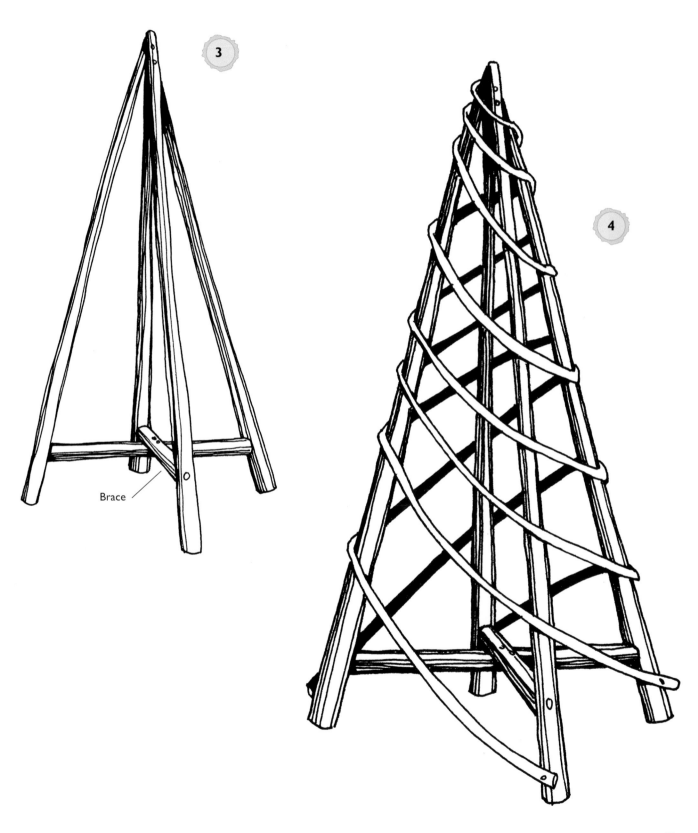

Brace

Angel Obelisk

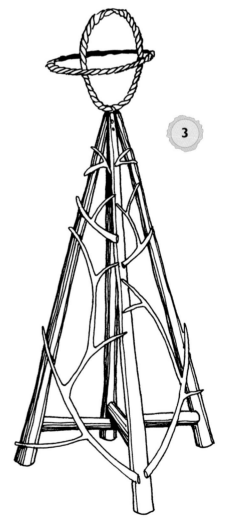

Adding a few vines and branches transforms an obelisk into an angel. The major difference is that I tend to make the angels shorter than other obelisks—usually about 5 feet tall. All you need are two 5-foot pieces of grapevine (half an inch or thinner for the head and halo), and two curved branches that are about the same size and shape for the wings.

Step 1: Build a basic obelisk and decorate it with branches, twigs, or vines.

Step 2: To make the angel's head: Create a crossed circle in the center of a 5-foot piece of grapevine. Take one of the ends and loop it through the circle, over and over, until you get to the end of the vine. (You might only get a couple of loops.) Do the same with the other end. Push the head into shape, oval or round, as you wish. Fasten it to the obelisk frame with a couple of small screws.

Step 3: Repeat this process to make a halo. Fasten the halo to the head with wire.

Step 4: Find two branches long enough to extend beyond the obelisk frame in curves that give the impression of wings. Drill pilot holes and drive screws to fasten the wings to the frame.

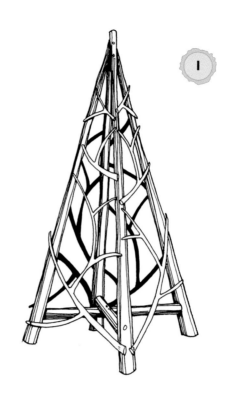

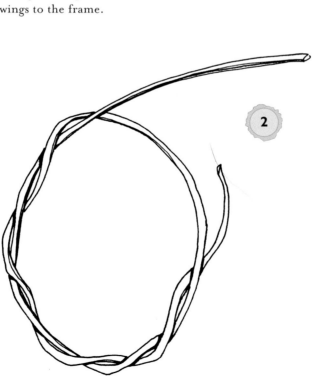

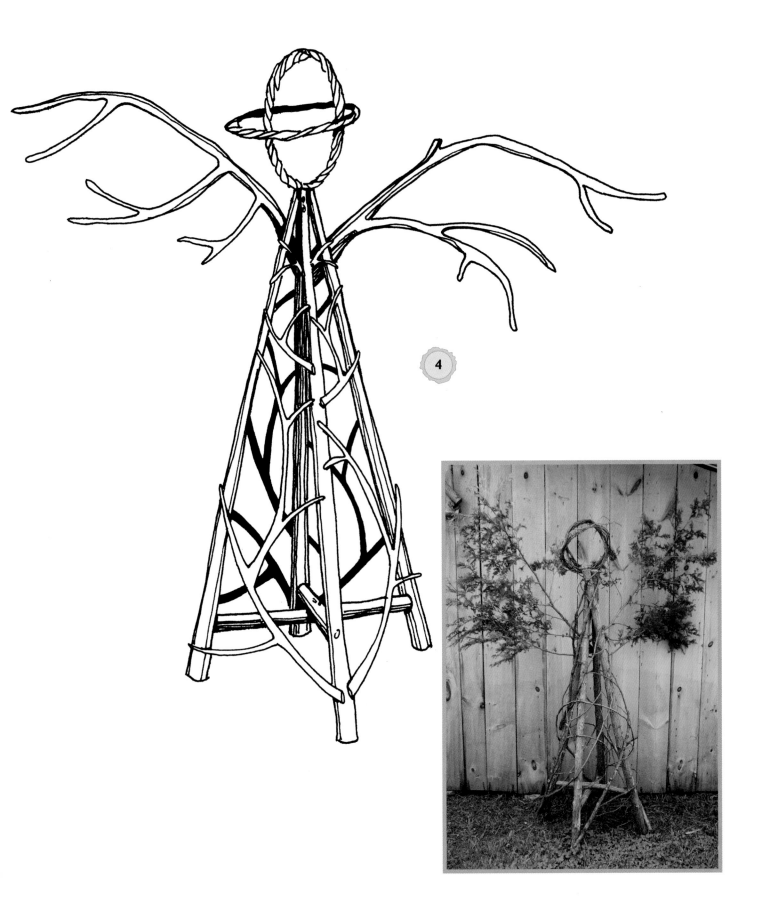

4

Long Planter

This planter is more like a two-tier shelf for a container garden. When you choose plants for it, you might include some trailing or twining varieties, and then train the vines through and around the decorative branches.

I think rough-cut lumber looks best for the shelf boards, but use whatever you have on hand. Use cedar or some other weather-resistant lumber if the planter will be exposed to rain or snow.

Speaking of snow, in the winter you could fill the planter with spruce tops and add twinkling lights. A few dried red berries or some holly sprigs would add another festive touch.

Tools:

- Power drill
- Saw
- Hammer
- Pruning shears
- Staple gun

Materials:

- (4) Legs: straight poles, 36" long, 1½" to 2" in diameter
- (10) 10" Crosspieces: straight branches, 1" in diameter
- (4) Shelf boards: 1 × 5 boards, 32" long
- (2) Top rails: straight branches 1" in diameter, 34" to 36" long
- (2) Top trim: 34" straight pieces
- (2) Bottom trim: 32" straight pieces
- Decorative branches
- Assorted nails, screws, and staples

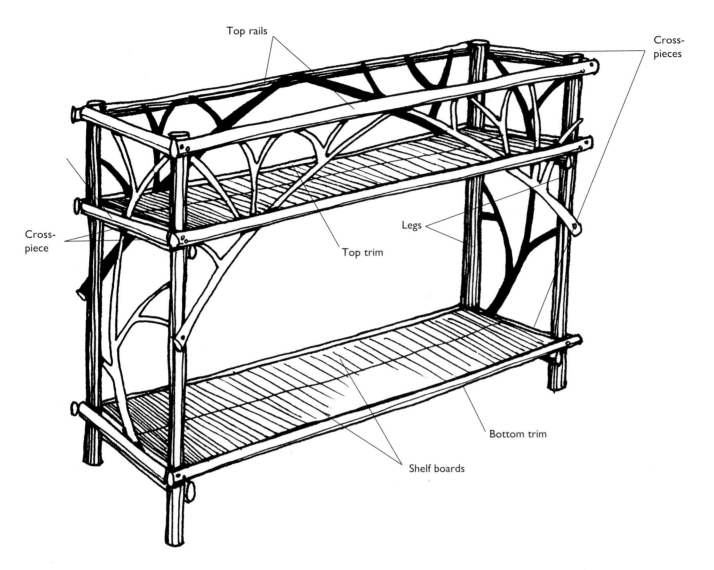

Top rails

Cross-pieces

Cross-piece

Legs

Top trim

Bottom trim

Shelf boards

Step 1: Arrange two 36" legs and two 10" crosspieces in a rough rectangle. Place the top crosspiece flush with the tops of the uprights and the bottom crosspiece about 4 inches above the ends. Add a third crosspiece 6 to 7 inches from the top. At each juncture, drill two pilot holes and drive a nail or screw into one hole of each pair. Adjust the framework until it's square, then add a second nail or screw at each juncture. Repeat this process to make a second frame.

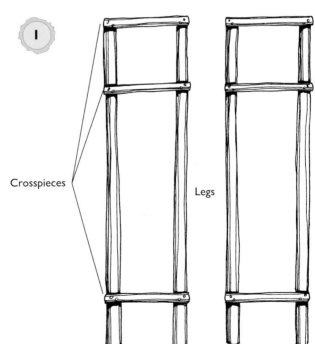

Crosspieces

Legs

Step 2: Lay a frame on a worktable with the cross-pieces facing down. Staple or nail interesting branches to each frame.

Step 3: Put a 10-inch crosspiece across the frame, directly above the bottom crosspiece on the other side. Place the remaining 10-inch piece 7 to 8 inches down from the top. Drill pilot holes and drive screws to attach these crosspieces. These are your shelf supports.

Step 4: Place two shelf boards between the two frames on the crosspieces at the bottom, and screw them into place, using two screws at the ends of each board to prevent warping. Repeat this process to add two boards to the upper crosspieces.

Step 5: Screw a scrap of wood into place temporarily to square the structure. Add a top rail to the front and back, connecting the frames to one another at the top. Drill pilot holes and drive screws into each juncture. Add a strong branch to each side of the frame. Drill pilot holes and drive screws into each juncture.

Step 6: Decorate the front and the back of the planter with branches and vines creating triangular bracing. (You may even want to add decorations across the top.) Remove the temporary brace you added in Step 5. Now, decorate the back. If your decoration pieces are flexible enough, loop them around one another, weave them through each other, or wrap them around the legs or top. If this is to be used indoors or on a porch protected from sun and rain, you might add other contrasting woods such as red osier dogwood or yellow willow.

Step 7: Place a 34-inch upper trim piece in front of the upper boards on each side. Drill pilot holes and attach the upper trim onto the legs. Put a 32-inch lower trim piece on the lower shelves. Attach it to the shelf boards.

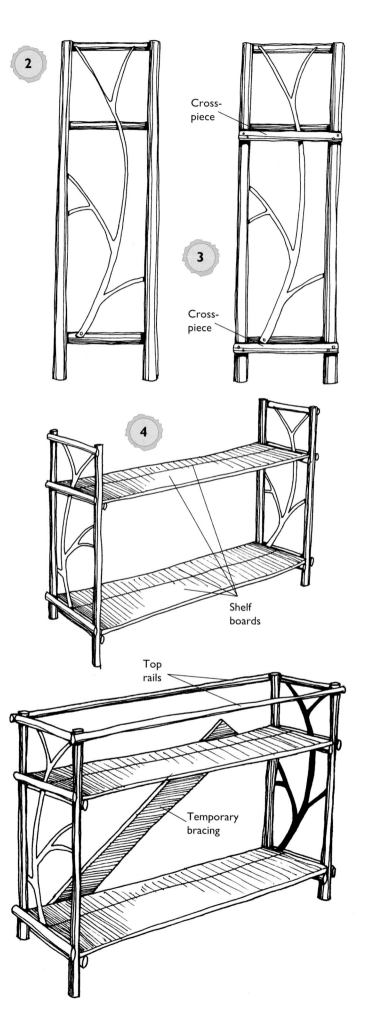

Cross-piece

Cross-piece

Shelf boards

Top rails

Temporary bracing

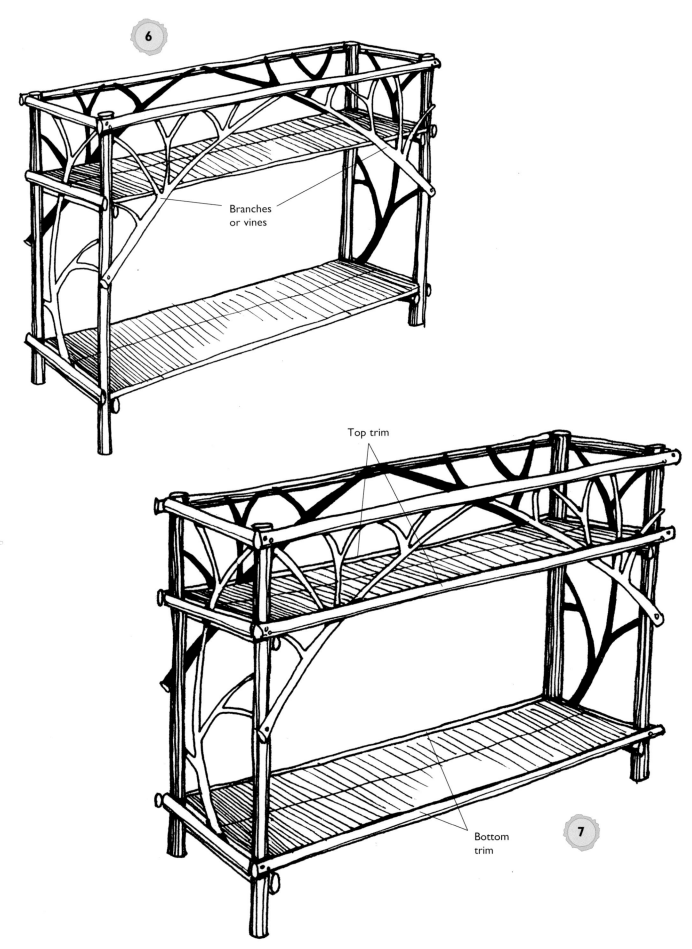

6

Branches
or vines

Top trim

Bottom
trim

7

Fence

When designing a fence, first consider your reasons for building it. Is it to create a visual separation of two spaces? To grow vines? If so, the decorative pieces have to be stronger than if the fence is purely decorative. Also, if you are going to be pulling dead vines off the fence each fall, it has to be strong enough to withstand that stress. Is the fence intended to confine animals? If so, it needs to be strong, and the spaces between the branches need to be small. (I am continually amazed at the small spaces that seemingly large animals can squeeze through.)

Step 1: Cut the rails to length. If you live in an area like I do, where rocks and boulders are numerous under the surface of the soil, your panels may have to differ in length to accommodate the soil conditions. If you are fortunate enough to have soil where the fence posts can be at regular intervals, you can select the spacing of the posts based on the way you want the fence to look. The limit is 6 to 8 feet, unless you are using rails that are quite heavy and will hold their shape over a long span. (If they are too thin, they will sag.) Lay out the rails, parallel to one another and space them to create the height you want. Arrange decorative branches and attach them to the rails. Depending on the size of the branches, staple them in place or drill pilot holes and use screws to attach the branches.

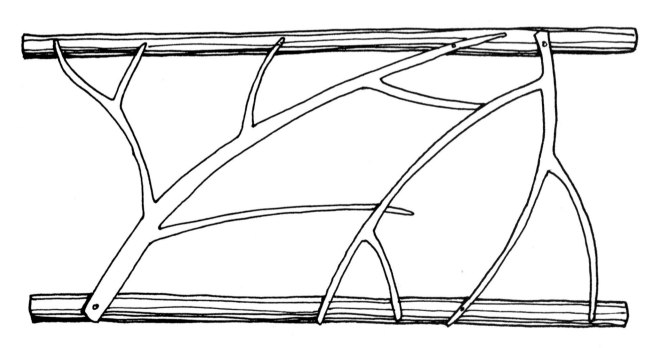

Step 2: Dig 3-foot holes and set the fence posts. When the posts are secure, prop the panels in place, drill pilot holes, and attach the rails to the posts with heavy screws.

If you are trying to install the posts in bedrock, holes really aren't a very good option. Instead, support the posts with posts that are angled in from the four directions and either wired or screwed into place. (This uses the logic of the patent fences that are common in our part of Ontario.)

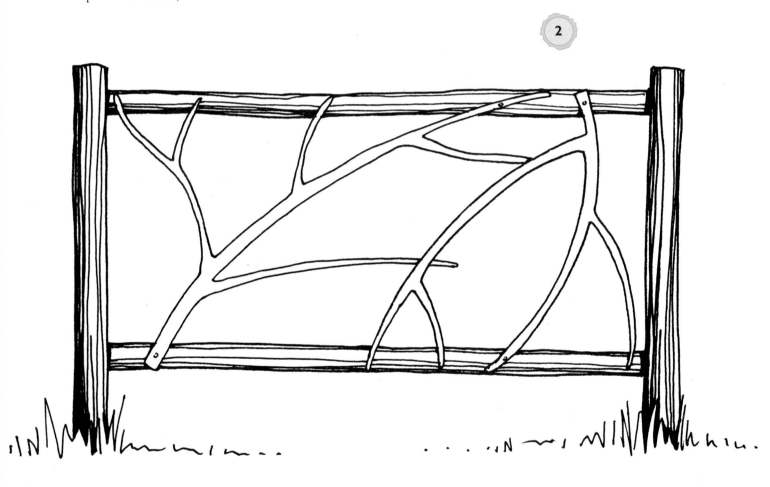

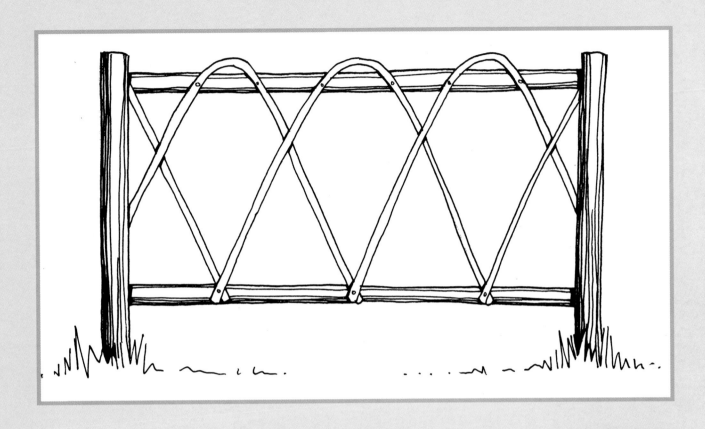

Here are some common decorative variations for your fencing panels: a zig-zag using vines or bent branches, and a radiating pattern using straight branches.

Gate

A gate needs to be built to suit its purpose. For example, the length of the posts depends how tall you want the gate and whether its purpose is functional or purely decorative. At our house, we are always trying to keep the deer out of our garden, so by necessity our gates are tall. A gate makes a wonderful add-on to a rustic fence or arbor.

Step 1: Measure the opening for the gate. Subtract about an inch from this measurement to allow the gate to fit comfortably into the opening. Remember to allow for lumps and bumps that may be on the fence or gate posts. Select or cut a bottom piece and a top piece to fit this measurement. (The bottom piece needs to be fairly straight, but the top piece can be straight, arched, or any interesting shape you can find.) Position the posts to fit the opening, and place the top and bottom pieces between them. At each juncture, drill two pilot holes as far apart as possible. Put one screw in at each juncture and adjust the framework until it is square. When all is ready, put a second screw in each juncture.

Step 2: Choose strong branches to decorate the gate. (Keep in mind that a gate needs strong triangular bracing to keep it from sagging. It is especially important to include a strong piece that runs from the bottom corner of the hinged side diagonally to the top corner on the opposite side.) Drill pilot holes and drive screws to attach the branches to the gate's framework. Next, find several places where strong branches cross each other, and attach the branches to one another at those joints. This technique, which will add to the strength of the gate, is especially useful if you are creating a lattice.

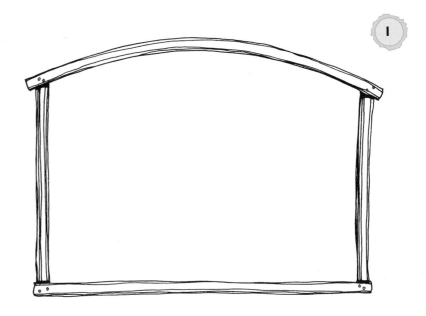

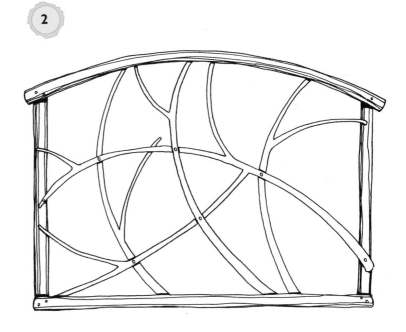

Tools:

- Power drill
- Hammer
- Pruning saw
- Pruning shears
- Staple gun

Materials:

- (2) Posts: of desired height
- (1) Bottom rail: for width at bottom of gate
- Decorative branches
- (1) Top rail: straight or curved piece for top
- Assorted screws, nails, and staples

(below) This two-door gate pivots from both sides, opening from the middle. Each door of the gate uses two posts of different lengths, with a curved piece that joins the posts and forms the rounded portion. It was built by one of my students, Brenda Conboy.

ॐ (above) This gate in my garden uses a
   crosshatch pattern of small, straight
   pieces to fill the space between the
   posts and rails.

Arbor

An arbor is an ambitious project, but entirely possible after you've prac-
ticed on smaller pieces. Read through all the instructions, including the
variations at the end, before you begin work. After all the time and effort
you've put into this arbor, you'll want it to fit your own vision of style as
well as your home and yard.

Many people use the arbor as part of an ensemble that includes a
rustic fence and gate.

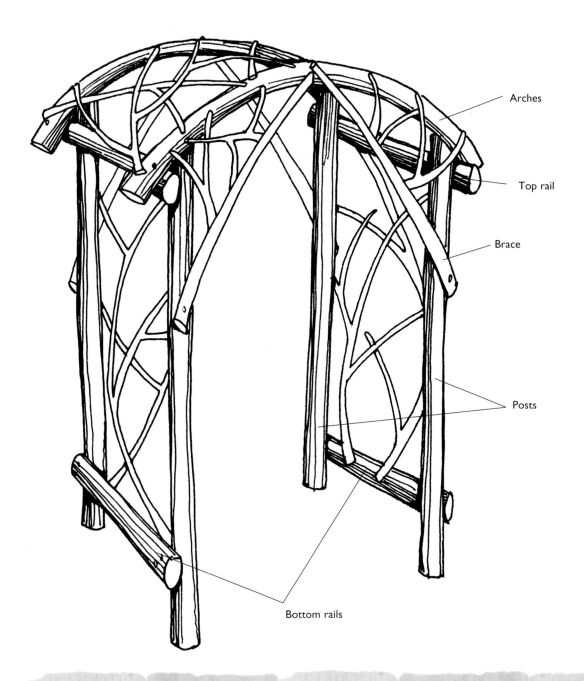

Arches

Top rail

Brace

Posts

Bottom rails

Tools:

- Power drill
- Pruning saw
- Pruning shears
- Hammer
- Staple gun

Materials:

- (4) Posts: 2" to 4" in diameter, 6 ft. long
- (2) Top rails: 1½" to 2" in diameter, 31" long
- (2) Arches: matching, curved, strong branches of desired length
- (2) Bottom rails: 2" to 3" in diameter, 27" long
- (4) Braces: slightly angled, strong branches, cut to length
- Scrap lumber for temporary bracing
- Heavy branches for decoration
- Assorted nails, screws, and staples

Step 1: Lay one pair of posts out on your work-surface. Place a 27-inch bottom rail about 6 inches up from the bottom and the 31-inch top rail 2-3 inches down from the top. The top post should overlap the sides by about 2 inches. At each joint, drill two pilot holes, placing them as far apart as possible. Drive a nail or screw into one hole at each joint. At this point, square up your framework and put in the remaining four nails or screws. Repeat this process to build the framework for the other side of the arbor.

Step 2: Turn one frame over so that the rails are on the bottom and the posts are on top. Decorate the frame with branches, attaching them with nails, screws, and staples. If possible, screw the branches to each other one or two times. Repeat on second frame.

Step 3: Lay the frames on their sides with the rails on the outside. Select two straight or matching arched pieces for the top. (These will determine the width of your arbor.) Cut two braces from your scrap lumber about 5 inches shorter than the top pieces, and a shorter brace to go between them. If you are working alone, tie each framework to a support (I use chairs) so the arches fit into their spaces at the top and the braces fit across the bottom. (These braces have a two-fold purpose: One is to maintain the correct shape of the arbor as you work on it, and the other is to provide strength and support when you transport the arbor to its final destination.) Screw the braces to the bottom of the arbor and square it up so your top and bottom rails are perpendicular to the ground (not leaning one way or the other). Use the shorter brace to hold everything in place. Then make sure that your four main posts are square to the braces. At the top, secure the two arches with strong nails or screws to both the posts and the braces.

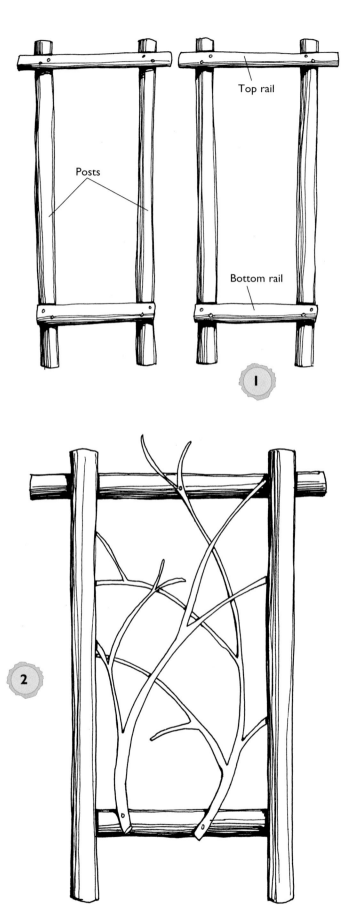

Arches

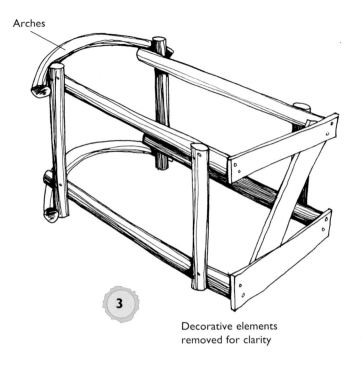

3

Decorative elements
removed for clarity

Braces

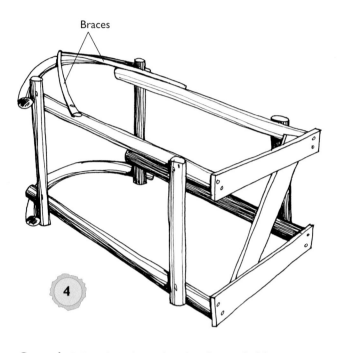

4

Top decorations

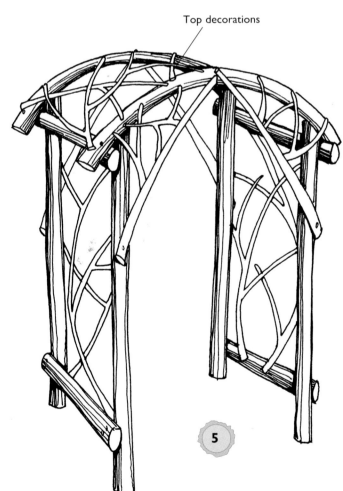

5

Step 4: Select four branches for the angled braces. (These can be straight, curved, or twisted, but must be strong.) Put two braces on the upper side of the arbor, measuring up from the bottom of the posts to see that they are equally placed on their heavy ends. Measure to the center of the top piece and mark it: This will be where you attach the top ends. Attach these braces with strong nails or screws. Decorate the space between each piece and the main framework. (This is both for esthetics and for additional strength.) Roll the entire piece over and do the same on the other side.

Step 5: If you want, you can pull the ends of your four support braces and attach them to either the arch on the other side or to the top crosspiece of the side of the framework. If this doesn't nicely fill in the space, add another piece or two across the top. For a different look, you can cut off the tops of the four tri-angular supports where they go past the arches and decorate the top with separate branches. The first technique gives you a domed effect as it extends the arbor upwards. The second technique gives you a somewhat flat surface along the plane of the arches. When you have installed the arbor in the yard or gar-den, remove the temporary braces from the bottom.

❧ (left) This arbor uses straight pieces for decorative fill between the posts and a pair of diagonal braces on each upper corner. This is the garden of Andy Fisher and Jill Dunkley.

❧ (below) Front and back views of the same arbor at the home of Jeff and Chantale Woodrow. This style makes use of the extra-long corner braces wrapped up and over the top of the arbor, as described in the last step on page 83. Notice how this arbor breaks up the monotony of the plain brick walls and serves to frame the window when viewed from one direction, and the ornamental tree from the other direction.

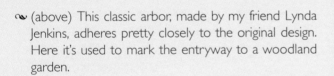 (above) This classic arbor, made by my friend Lynda Jenkins, adheres pretty closely to the original design. Here it's used to mark the entryway to a woodland garden.

(right) This variation is built with strongly geometric lines, including decorative lattice panels in the spaces between the posts which match similar lattice work used elsewhere in the garden. This arbor, at the home of Mark Zubak and Heather Budgell, invites you onto a path through the woods.

Potting Bench

This bench was designed at a convenient height for potting and given shelves to store pots and tools, but the basic design can be used for many things. I have seen it used as a wine rack at my daughter's wedding, a china cabinet at a customer's house, and a display unit in retail stores.

The way you intend to use the piece will dictate the dimensions, to some extent. Read through the directions here and tailor the design to fit your needs. Really, this is just an enlarged version of the garden shelf (page 94) with more and different shelves.

Tools:

- Power drill
- Saw

- Pruning shears
- Hammer

- Staple gun

Materials:

- (2) Rear legs: 1½" to 2" in diameter, 68" long
- (2) Front legs: 1½" to 2" in diameter, 38" long
- (6) Long rails: 1" to 1½" in diameter, 24" long
- (2) Short rails: 1" to 1½" in diameter, 6" long

- (2) Top shelf supports: 1" to 1½" in diameter, curved branch
- (8) Shelf boards: 1 × 6 cedar boards, 42" long
- (1) Top rail: curved branch, 1½" in diameter, about 46" long

- Decorative branches
- (4) Trim pieces: 1" in diameter, cut to fit
- Assorted nails, screws, and staples

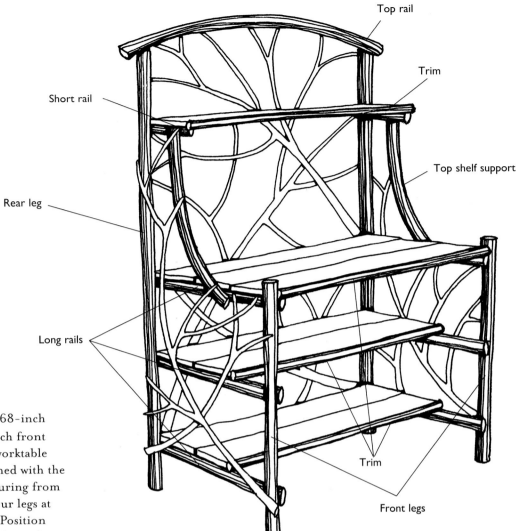

Top rail

Trim

Short rail

Top shelf support

Rear leg

Long rails

Trim

Front legs

Step 1: Start with two 68-inch rear legs and two 38-inch front legs. Put the legs on a worktable with their bottoms aligned with the edge of the table. Measuring from the bottom, mark all four legs at 7", 22", 37", and 58". Position one front and one rear leg to be the sides of the frame, placing 24-inch long rails between them just below the 7", 22", and 37" marks. (These are your shelf supports.) At each juncture drill two pilot holes and drive a screw into one of the holes. Make sure the frame is square, and then drive a second screw into each juncture. Add a 6-inch short rail at the 58-inch mark. Attach a curved top shelf support between this piece and the first long rail. Repeat this process to make a second frame that is the mirror image of the first.

Step 2: Staple decorative branches and twigs onto the frames. These go on the outside (shelf supports are on the inside).

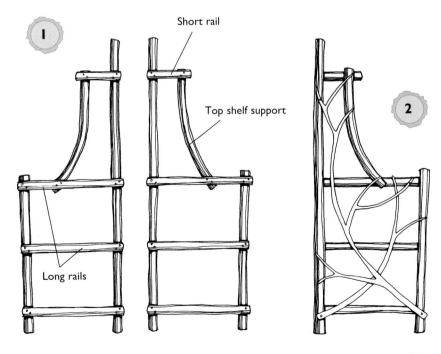

1

Short rail

Top shelf support

2

Long rails

Step 3: Prop the frames up so the rails are on the inside and the rear legs (the back of the potting bench) are facing you. (You will need to recruit helpers to hold the frames or find a way to support them while you work.) Lay a shelf board across the bottom long rails; drill two pilot holes into each end and drive screws through the board and into the rails. Check to make sure the piece is square. Add a second shelf board between the rails at the top at the marked 37" height. Position a strong decorative branch running diagonally from the lower corner on one side to the upper corner on the other. This acts as a brace to hold the piece in shape. Drill pilot holes and screw the branch in place, attaching it at all main junctures. As you work, make sure that the two side frames are perpendicular to the surface you're working on.

Step 4: Place the curved top rail on the back, joining the two rear legs. (This piece can sit on top of the legs or in front of them.) When the top is secured, add 1 × 6s to the center and top long rails.

Step 5: Decorate the back of the potting bench. For added strength, attach the decorative branches to each other and to the 1 × 6s whenever possible.

Step 6: Working from the front of the piece, attach the remaining shelf boards. (I sometimes make the bottom two shelves shallower to allow more leg room.) Trim the front of the shelves with long, thin branches. Use trim nails or screws to fasten the branches in place.

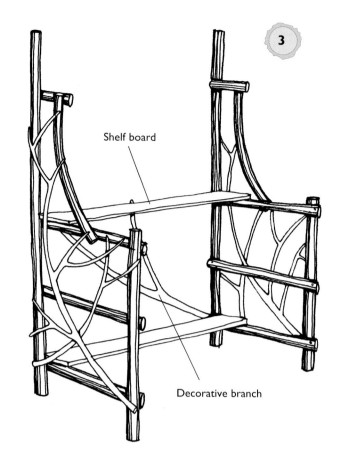

Shelf board

Decorative branch

3

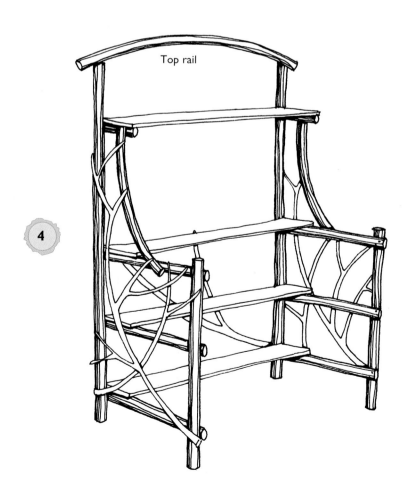

Top rail

4

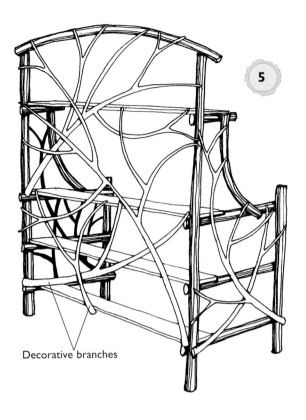

(5)

Decorative branches

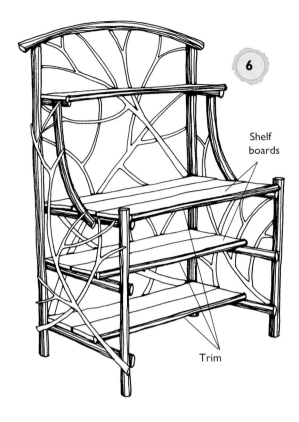

(6)

Shelf boards

Trim

☙ This garden shelf variation
found at Rideau Nursery in
Grower, Ontario, is narrower,
to fit a confined space, but
deeper to maintain an ample
amount of storage space. A
second upper shelf is also
added.

Shaker Stool

The top of a stool like this traditionally is woven with black ash or white oak stripping, which can be found in many craft supply stores. You can also use Shaker tape, a sturdy cloth tape available in several colors, also available in craft supply stores. I use cooked bark, peeled in midsummer from freshly cut trees. I then soak it, so it is easy to weave and provides a sturdy woven top.

If you're up for a challenge, harvest black ash or white oak for your stool. Both black ash and white oak are labor intensive to prepare. Black ash logs must be pounded to loosen the growth rings which then can be dried, soaked, and cut. White oak is split with an axe and then a hammer and froe once it has been cut into logs. Afterwards, it is smoothed with a spoke shave on a shaving horse.

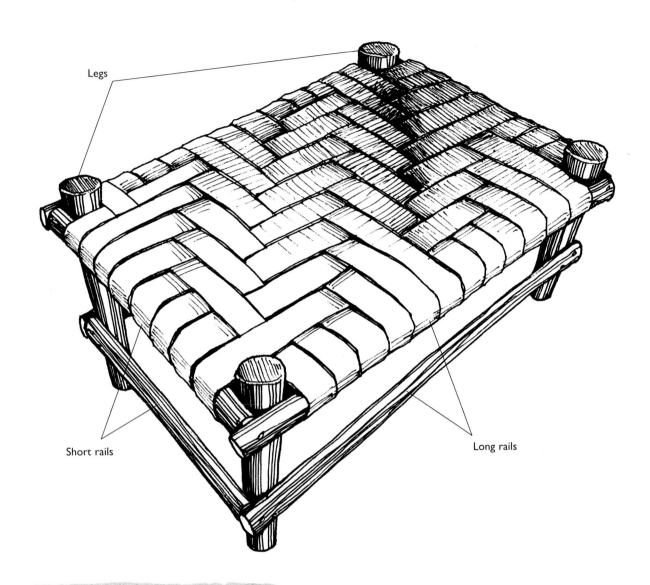

Legs

Short rails

Long rails

Tools:

- Power drill
- Saw
- Pruning shears
- Staple gun
- Utility knife
- Standard stapler
- Scissors

Materials:

- (4) Legs: 1½" to 2" in diameter, 12" long
- (4) Long rails: 1½" to 2" in diameter, 18" long
- (4) Short rails: 1½" to 2" in diameter, 12" long
- Strips of black ash, white oak, cedar bark, Shaker tape, about ½" wide

Step 1: Line up the ends of the 12-inch legs with the edge of a worktable. Mark each leg about an inch from the top and 2 to 3 inches up from the bottom. Position a short rail on a pair of legs above the 2- to 3-inch mark; drill two pilot holes as far apart as possible at each juncture, and drive a screw into one of these holes. Make sure your framework is square, and then drive a second screw into each juncture. Repeat this process with the other pair of legs. (The rails could also be attached to the insides of the legs, as you see in the photo on page 90—but I find this way easier to square up.)

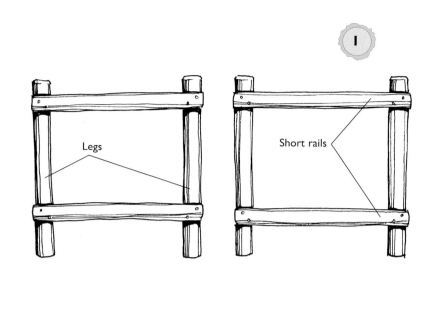

Step 2: Prop the two frames on their sides, with the rails on the outside. Position a long rail level with each lower short rail; attach the long rails to the end of the short rails with one screw. Stand the frame up so it is straight and add a second screw to each joint.

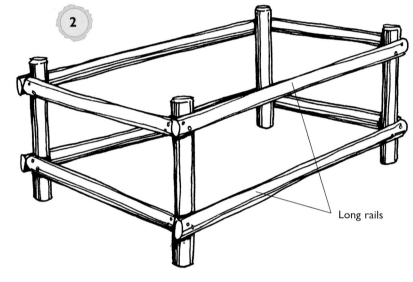

Step 3: Fasten one long strip to the outside of the top of the frame, using one or two staples. (Use a staple gun with flat staples as opposed to rounded ones.) Wrap the strip across the top, down around the same crosspiece, and come up across the top.

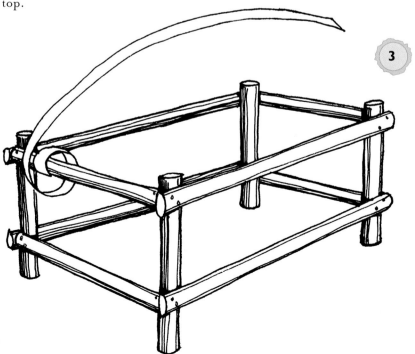

Step 4: Pull the strip across to the other side of the stool, around the top piece, and across the bottom, next to the beginning. Continue in this manner until you have filled in the space across the top of the stool. Keep the strips evenly taut—not too tight, not too loose—and leave a tiny gap between each strip. If you need to join another strip, put the new strip over the end of the old, overlapping them by about 3 inches. Staple the strips together, using a standard stapler. (Staple from the top down and make sure the back of the staple will be inside the weaving.) Complete this step by coming across the top of the stool. Wrap the strip around the outside of the crosspiece, under your work, behind the leg and out the front, still on the bottom of the piece.

Step 5: Now you're ready to weave both top and bottom in a herringbone weave, an over 3/under 3 pattern, alternating by one strip each subsequent row. That is to say, Row One is over 3/under 3. Row Two starts with over 2 and continues with under 3/over 3. Row Three starts with over 1. Row Four starts with under 3, next—under 2, next—under 1, and so on. You are weaving both top and bottom. Do not end a strip at an edge. When a strip ends, take another and overlap it by several inches, weaving the two as if they were one. (When using ash, oak, or cedar, it's best to weave the whole seat in one sitting. If you do take a break, put the strips back in the water while you're away from the project.) Keep your top wet. When you are finished, remove any staples that show.

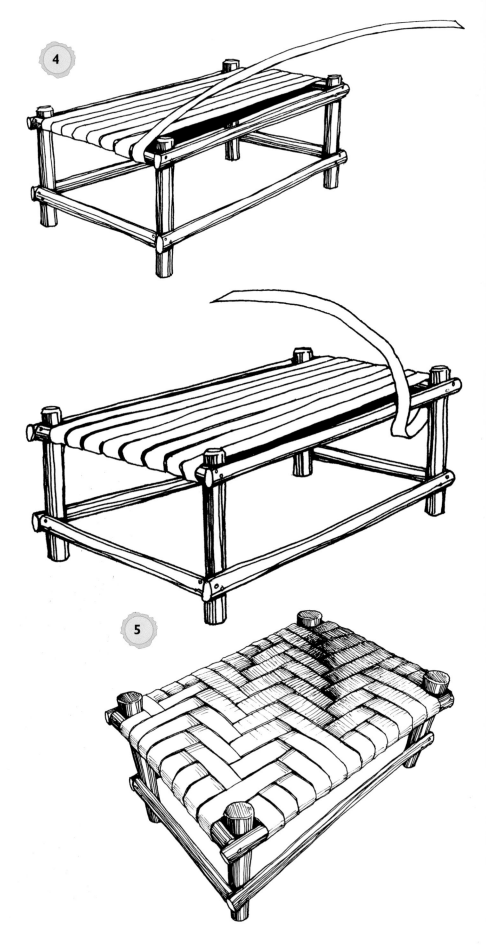

Garden Shelf

These instructions can be adapted to make any shelves you want, from shoe racks to baker's racks. When making outdoor furniture, use cedar lumber. Otherwise, any lumber will do—including strong plywood. If you have any old, weathered lumber, this shelf is a good way to use it.

Many of my students, though, use this piece as an indoor nightstand or end table.

For stability, make sure that the decorative pieces, filling the spaces between the legs and rails, offer diagonal support.

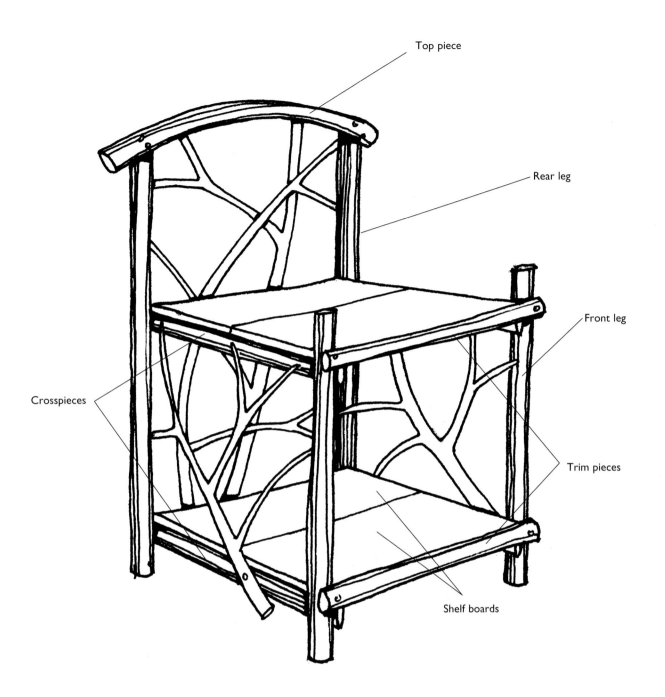

Top piece

Rear leg

Front leg

Trim pieces

Crosspieces

Shelf boards

Tools:

- Power drill
- Hammer
- Saw
- Pruning shears
- Staple gun

Materials:

- (2) Rear legs: 1½" in diameter, 30" long
- (2) Front legs: 1½" in diameter, 24" long
- (4) Crosspieces: 1½" in diameter, 12" long
- (4) Shelf boards: 1 × 6 boards, 18" long
- (1) Top piece, decorative branch, about 22" long
- (2) Trim pieces: 1" in diameter, approximately 20" long
- Decorative branches
- Assorted nails, screws, and staples

Step 1: Place a rear leg and front leg on your worktable, lined up with the edge and 12 inches apart. Place one crosspiece about an inch from the top of the front leg and 7 inches down from the top of the rear leg. Place another crosspiece about 3 inches up from the bottom of the legs. At each juncture, drill two pilot holes as far apart from each other as possible, taking care to only go through the top piece of wood. Drive a screw into one hole at each juncture. Make sure that the framework is square, and then put screws in the second holes. Create a second frame that is a mirror image of the first. (This is to say, if you made the first frame with the longer post on the left, now place it on the right and place the two shorter posts in opposite positions.)

Step 2: Place the frames on your work table with the 12-inch pieces lying on the table and the longer posts going upright on top of them. Decorate with small branches. Try to secure the main crossing branches in at least one place.

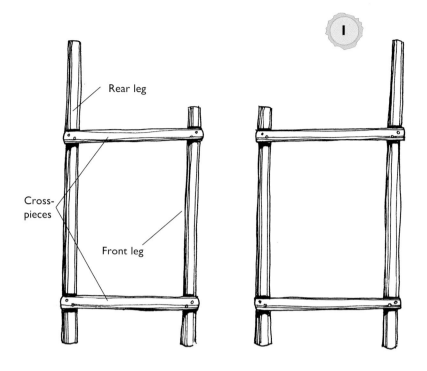

Rear leg

Cross-pieces

Front leg

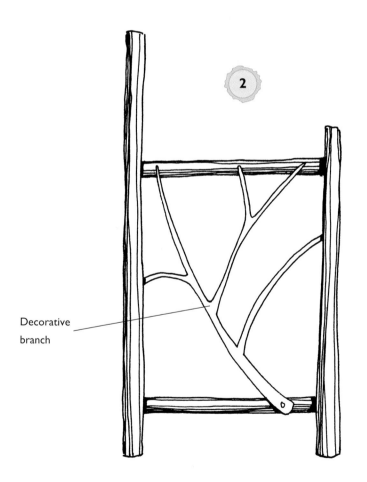

Decorative branch

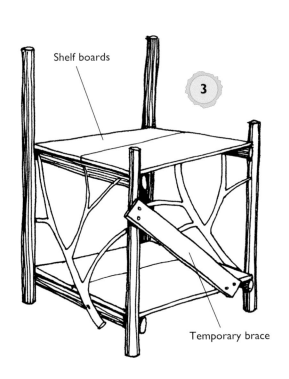

Shelf boards

3

Temporary brace

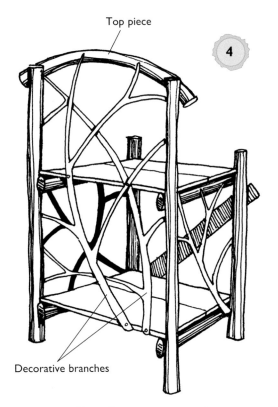

Top piece

4

Decorative branches

5

Trim pieces

Step 3: Stand the two frames upright, aligning the front legs with the front edge of the table. Place the frames 18 inches apart with the crosspieces facing each other. (If you don't have anyone to help, you may need to tie the frames to something or prop them against something.) Place four shelf boards on the crosspieces, forming the shelves. Drill pilot holes and screw these boards into place. Place 2 screws into each end of each board to prevent warping. Brace the assembly with a scrap board running diagonally from one corner of the shelf to the other front leg, making sure that it is upright and not leaning one way or the other.

Step 4: Turn the unit around so it's facing you, and put a decorative piece across the top. Add decorative branches to the back. These can be on top of, or in front of, the back legs. Fasten the main part of at least one branch to each shelf to provide bracing support.

Step 5: Remove the brace from the front, and then add a trim piece to the front of each shelf.

Bent Twig Stool

With its bent twig sides, this stool makes a perfect complement to the chair shown on page 116. No matter what you pair it with, a stool like this makes a nice place to rest your weary feet.

If you're going to use the stool indoors, willow and basswood twigs are good choices. For an outdoor setting, cedar works well, although it is less flexible and will need to be worked more. Before you begin adding the twigs, trim them well and "work the spite out of them." This means carefully bending the thicker ends, moving towards the thinner ends to soften the fibers so the twigs bend more easily.

Tools:

- Power drill
- Saw
- Pruning shears
- Rasp

Materials:

- (4) Legs: 1½ to 2" in diameter, 12" long
- (4) Short rails, 1½" in diameter, 9" long
- (4) Long rails, 1½" in diameter, 18" long
- (7 to 10) Seat slats: ¾" in diameter, cut to fit
- (8) Pliable twigs, about ½" thick, 36" long
- Assorted screws

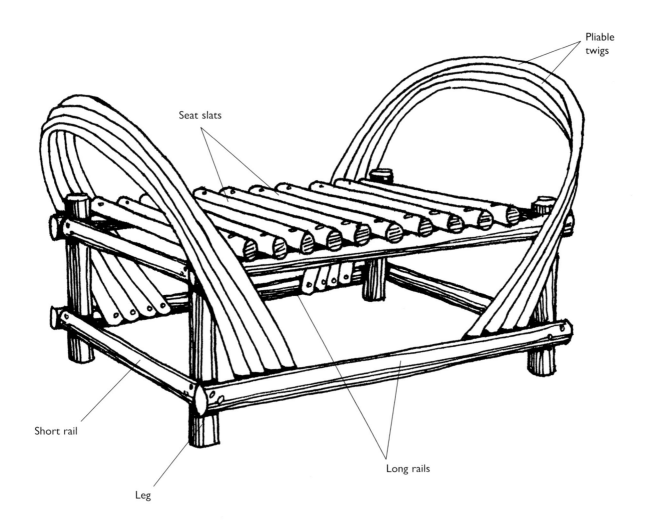

Pliable twigs

Seat slats

Short rail

Leg

Long rails

Step 1: Use a rasp to soften the top edges of the four legs. Next, place two of the legs on the table, even with the front edge of the table and 9 inches apart. Place one of the short rails 1 inch down from the top of the legs and the other 3 to 4 inches up from the bottom. At each juncture, drill two pilot holes; drive a screw or nail into one hole at each juncture. Adjust the framework and then add a second nail or screw to each juncture. Repeat to make a second frame identical to the first.

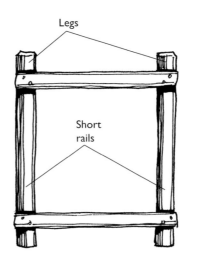

Legs

Short rails

1

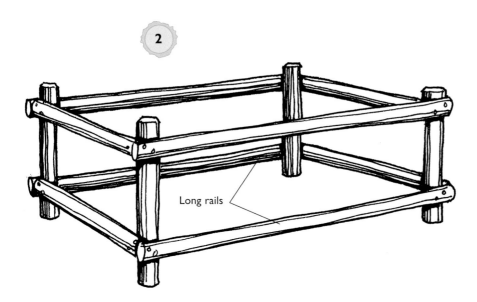

Step 2: Use four long rails to connect the two frameworks at the level of the short rail. Drill two pilot holes at each juncture and drive one screw through the long rail and into the end of the short rail. Stand the stool up on a worktable and adjust it until all four legs sit on the table and are perpendicular to it. Finally, drive a second screw into each juncture.

Long rails

Step 3: Select eight pieces for the bent-twig work. They should be about 36" long, about half an inch thick, and very flexible (take the spite out of them). Place the butt (larger) end of one of these twigs behind the bottom rail on the long side of the stool, right next to the leg. Drill a pilot hole and screw the twig in place. Gently bend the twig to the outsides of the top rails, then behind the opposite bottom rail until the other end reaches the corresponding place on the opposite side of the stool. Drill a pilot hole and attach the end of the twig to the leg of the stool. Adjust the twig until the arch is even.

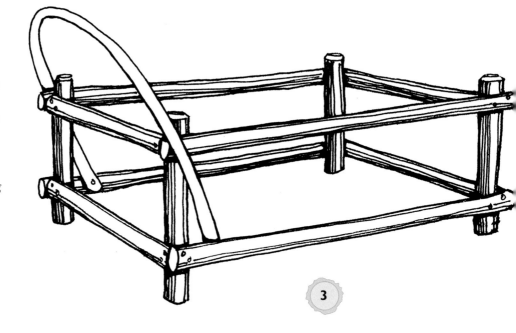

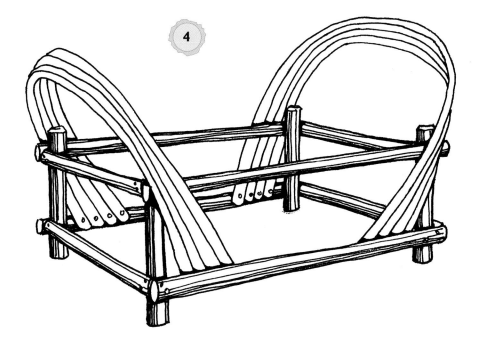

Step 4: Put the butt end of a second twig on the side that has the small end of the previous twig. Attach the second twig to the first with small screws as you bend it across to the other side. You will start and end on a flat plane along the bottom rail. In the middle, your twig will be directly above the previous one. Add a third and fourth twig to this side. Repeat this process to attach four twigs to the other end of the stool. (Make sure the twigs are at the same height.)

Step 5: Cut 7 to 10 seat slats to fit, and space them evenly across the top of the stool to form a seat. Drill pilot holes and attach the ends of each twig to the top rails of the stool.

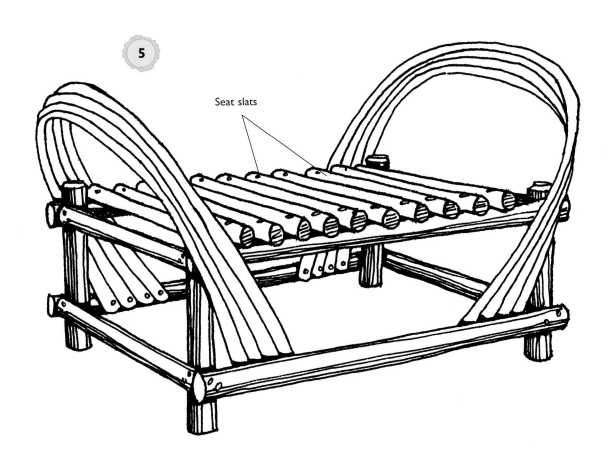

Seat slats

Coffee Table

Depending on how you plan to use your coffee table, choose either rough or planed boards for the top. Rough boards look more rustic and don't show spills and stains as much as planed boards. On the other hand, planed boards can be stained or painted, and have a more refined look.

For a different look, experiment with unusually shaped pieces for the legs or different patterns for the decorative sides.

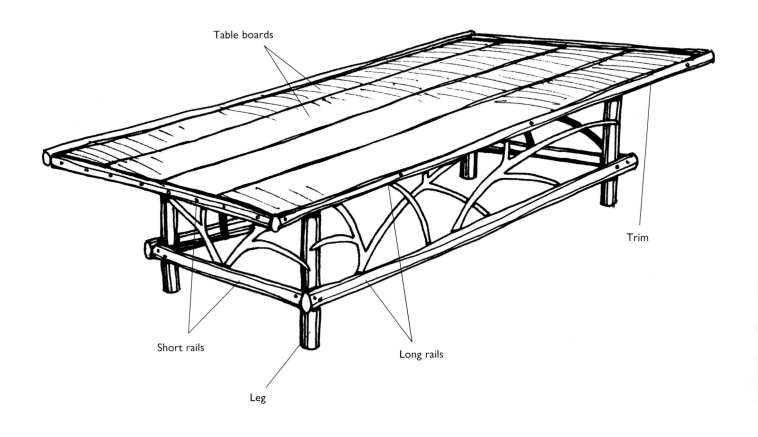

Table boards

Trim

Short rails

Leg

Long rails

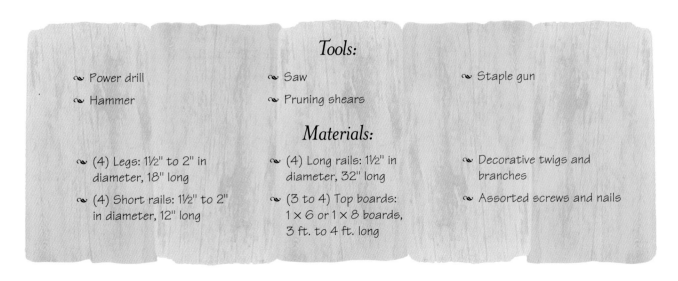

Tools:

- Power drill
- Hammer

- Saw
- Pruning shears

- Staple gun

Materials:

- (4) Legs: 1½" to 2" in diameter, 18" long

- (4) Short rails: 1½" to 2" in diameter, 12" long

- (4) Long rails: 1½" in diameter, 32" long

- (3 to 4) Top boards: 1 × 6 or 1 × 8 boards, 3 ft. to 4 ft. long

- Decorative twigs and branches

- Assorted screws and nails

Step 1: Arrange two legs and two short rails to form a frame. Fasten the upper rail flush with the tops of the legs and the lower one a few inches up from the bottom. Drill two pilot holes at each juncture, as far apart as possible. Drive only one screw into each juncture, and then adjust the frame and add the remaining screws. Repeat this process to make a second frame.

Step 2: Cut twigs and branches to fit the frames. Staple or screw them in place.

Step 3: Place the frames on their sides about 32 inches apart, with the rails on the outside. Position long rails against the ends of the short rails. At each juncture, drill two pilot holes and drive one screw into each juncture. Turn the piece over and do the same on the other side. Stand the assembly up and make sure that all four legs rest squarely on the ground. (To accomplish this, you may have to put downward pressure on some of the legs.) When the frame is solid, and straightened up, add a second screw to each juncture. Decorate the side frames with twigs and branches from the inside.

Step 4: Lay out the table boards and cut trim to fit across the ends and sides. Drill pilot holes and attach the branches to the table top, putting two screws into the end of each board.

Step 5: Put the top face down on a worktable and place the base on it. Drill pilot holes and attach the top to the base with two or three screws along each side and end.

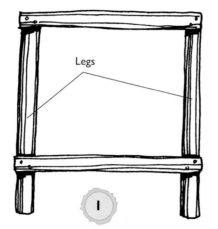

Legs

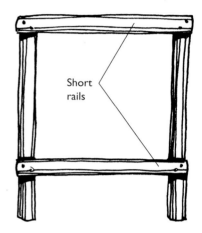

Short rails

1

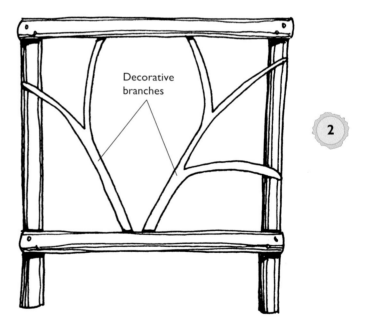

Decorative branches

2

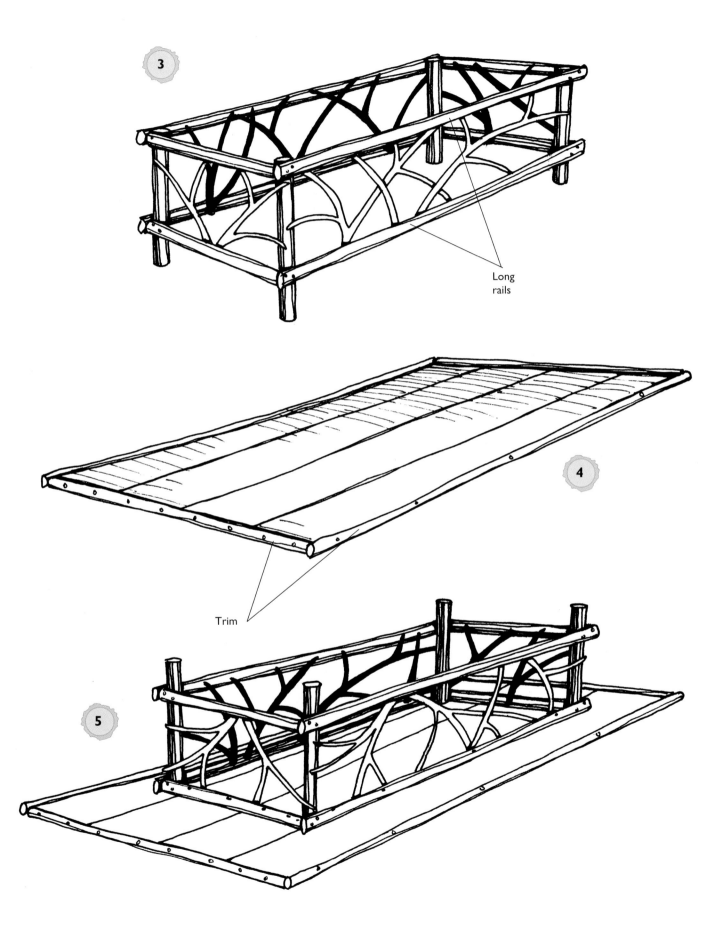

3

Long
rails

4

Trim

5

Cedar Table

A cedar table is among the most versatile projects you can build and also one of the easiest. In varying dimensions, the same basic design can become an end table, a night-stand, a dining table, or a console. Build one and soon you'll see dozens of possibilities.

Many people build several in various sizes to place around the garden. See the portfolio section of this book for examples of how this design can be used and how it can be adapted.

Step 1: Align the bases of two legs with the edge of a worktable. Take a 10-inch top rail and place it across the legs, flush with the tops and sides. Drill two pilot holes at each juncture and put in one screw at each. Take a 12-inch bottom rail and place it parallel to the edge of the table about 4 inches from the bottom of the legs. (The ends should be flush with the sides of the legs.) Fasten this branch in the same way as the first. Now adjust the shape so that the tops lean in evenly, and then add the second screws to the joints. Repeat this process to make a second frame.

Step 2: Put the frames on the table with the rails facing down and the legs up. Add decorative branches, stapling or screwing them in place. (Select and place the branches to strengthen the frames.)

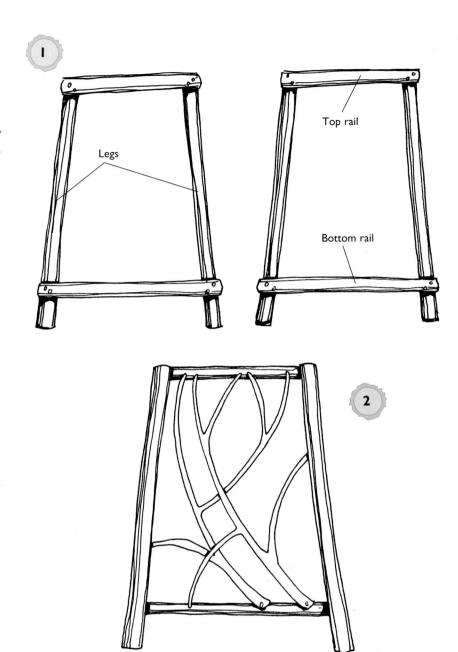

Legs

Top rail

Bottom rail

Tools:

- Power drill
- Hammer
- Saw
- Pruning shears
- Staple gun

Materials:

- (4) Legs: 1½" to 2" in diameter, 24" long
- (2) Top rails: 1" to 1½" in diameter, 10" long
- (2) Top rails: 1" to 1½" in diameter, 12" long
- (2) Bottom rails: 1" to 1½" in diameter, 12" long
- (2) Bottom rails: 1" to 1½" in diameter, 14" long
- (2) Table boards: 1 × 8 cedar, 16" long
- (4) Trim pieces: 1" in diameter, 18" long
- Decorative branches
- Assorted screws, nails, and staples

Step 3: Prop the frames in place, on their sides with the rails facing outwards. Place a top rail across the top of the frame, flush with the tops and sides of the legs. Drill two pilot holes at each juncture, but drive only one screw into each. Repeat this process to add a bottom rail to the frame, aligning it with the existing rails. Flip the base assembly over and do the same thing on the other side.

Step 4: Stand the table base on a flat surface. (It may be leaning to one side or another, or all four feet may not be touching the table.) Adjust the base assembly until it is stable and straight, and add the second screws to the various junctures.

Step 5: Working from the inside, add decorative branches to the two open sides.

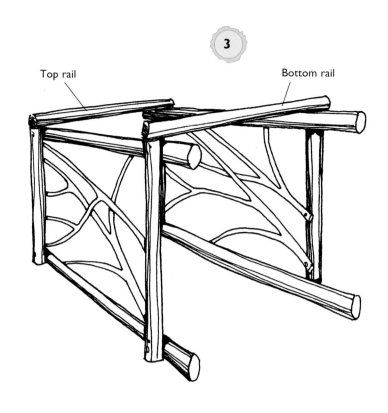

Top rail

Bottom rail

3

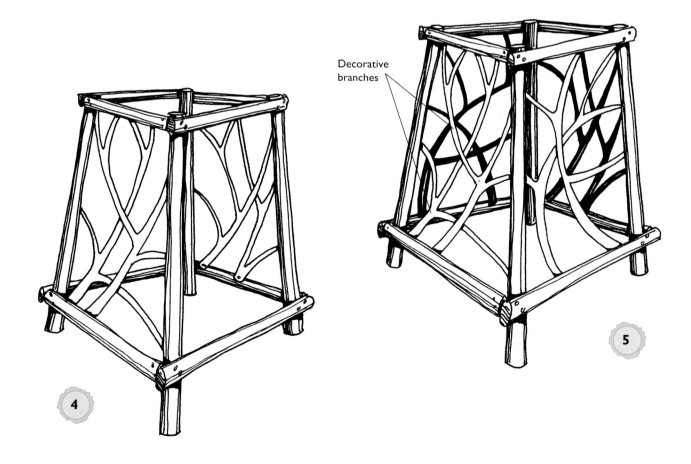

Decorative branches

4

5

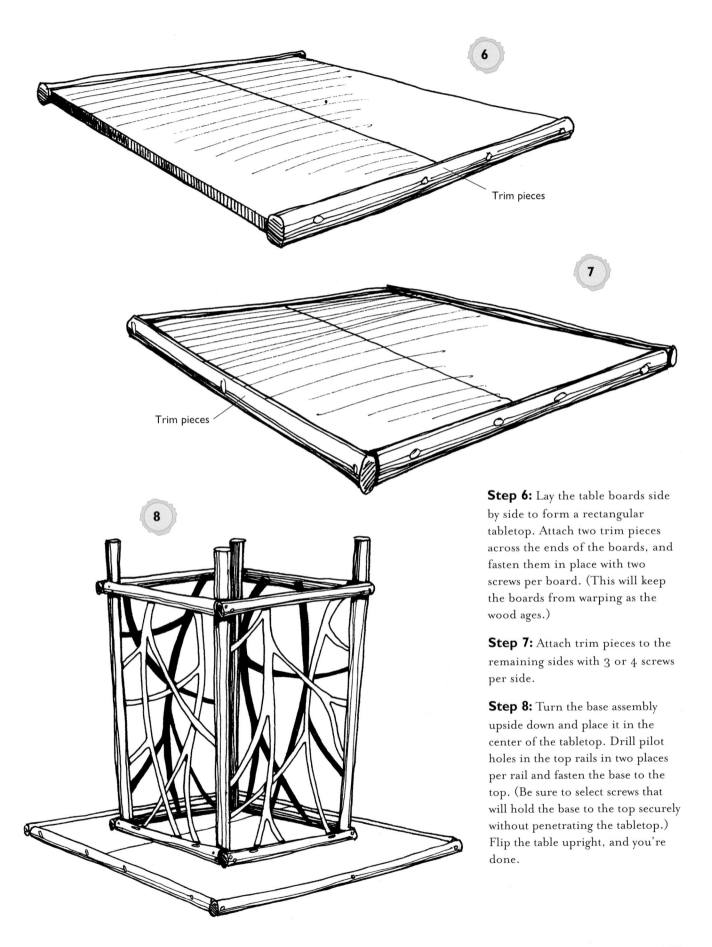

Trim pieces

Trim pieces

Step 6: Lay the table boards side by side to form a rectangular tabletop. Attach two trim pieces across the ends of the boards, and fasten them in place with two screws per board. (This will keep the boards from warping as the wood ages.)

Step 7: Attach trim pieces to the remaining sides with 3 or 4 screws per side.

Step 8: Turn the base assembly upside down and place it in the center of the tabletop. Drill pilot holes in the top rails in two places per rail and fasten the base to the top. (Be sure to select screws that will hold the base to the top securely without penetrating the tabletop.) Flip the table upright, and you're done.

Garden Bench

The design for this garden bench lends itself to many variations— you will see two examples on the last page of this project. You can easily shrink the design to create a chair-sized piece, or create different patterns for the back of the bench. For a more rustic look, you could form the seat from narrowly spaced branches rather than board slats, a variation used on the cover of this book. Use the design as a basis to explore your creativity and come up with your own designs.

The garden bench can be the anchor piece in an ensemble of garden furniture that could also include an arbor, a garden chair, and an end table or coffee table.

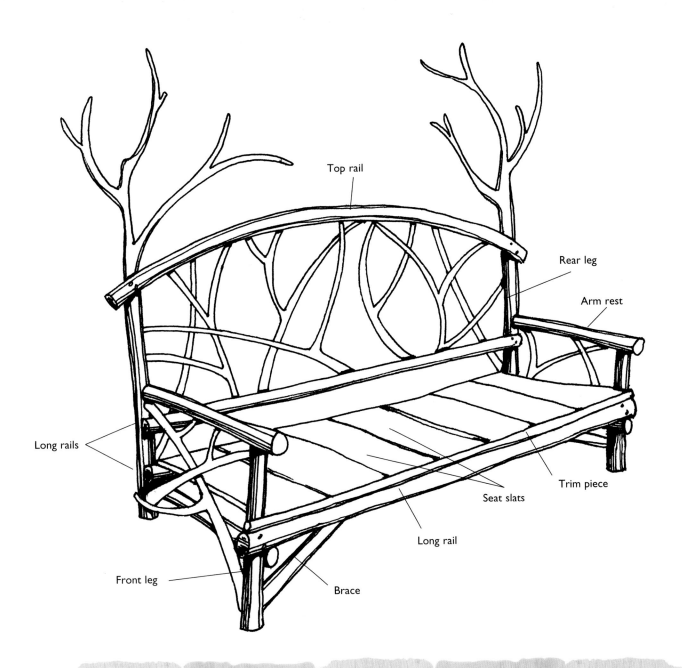

Top rail

Rear leg

Arm rest

Long rails

Trim piece

Seat slats

Long rail

Front leg

Brace

Tools:

- Power drill
- Cordless drill
- Pruning saw
- Pruning shears
- Hammer
- Staple gun

Materials:

- (2) Rear legs: small trees, 2" in diameter, 6 ft. tall
- (2) Front legs: 2" in diameter, 24" long
- (3) Long rails: 2" in diameter, 48" long
- (1) Curved top rail: 2" in diameter, 48" long
- (2) Short rails: 1½" in diameter, 22" long
- (2) Arm rests: 1½" in diameter, cut to length
- (2) Braces: cut to desired fit
- Decorative branches
- (1) Trim piece: 1" in diameter, 48" long
- (7) Seat slats: 1 × 6 cedar boards, cut to fit (about 18")
- Assorted nails, screws, and staples

Step 1: For the rear legs trim away the small branches from the sides of the chosen trees, using pruning shears. You can leave branches at the top for decoration if you like.

Position two long rails and the top rail against the rear legs. The bottom rails will be 16" and 24" from the bottom of the legs; the top rail, 32" from the bottom of the legs. The piece at 16" will need to be flat along the top surface where the seat will rest.

At each joint, drill two pilot holes as far apart as possible. Drive a deck screw into one of each pair of holes. Square up your structure and add the second nails or screws.

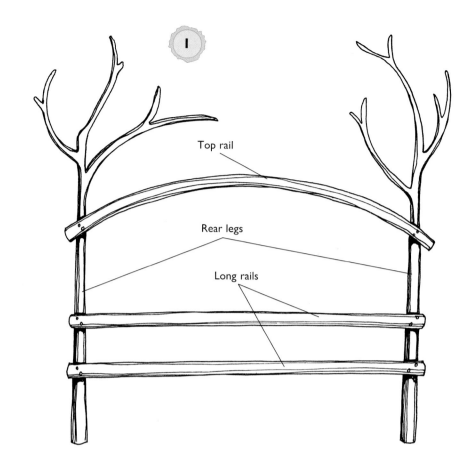

Top rail

Rear legs

Long rails

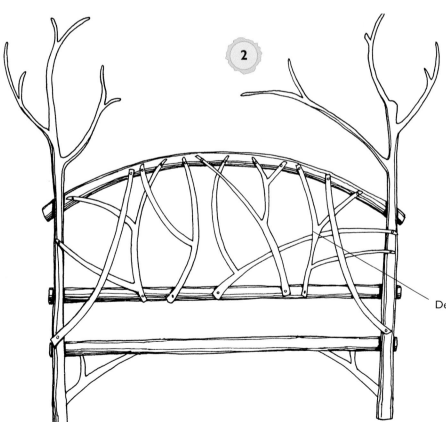

Step 2: Turn the workpiece over and add the decorative branches. For structural strength, make sure you provide strong triangular bracing within the framework and below the bottom rail. Drill pilot holes and attach all pieces with screws. You've now created the back of the bench; set it aside for now and construct the front. When you decorate, remember to keep it fairly flat for leaning comfort.

Decorative twigs

Step 3: To construct the front of the bench, position the last long rail over the front legs, 16" up from the bottom. Make sure the top of the crosspiece is slightly flattened, as the seat will rest on it.

Drill two pilot holes, then secure the rail to the legs with a single screw on each side. Square up the front assembly, then drive the other deck screws.

Position the cross braces against the front sides of the front legs and rails, drill pilot holes, and attach with deck screws.

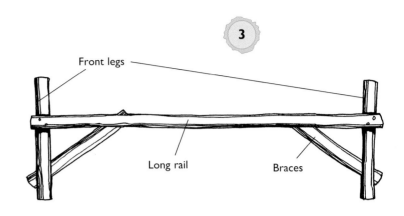

Front legs

Long rail

Braces

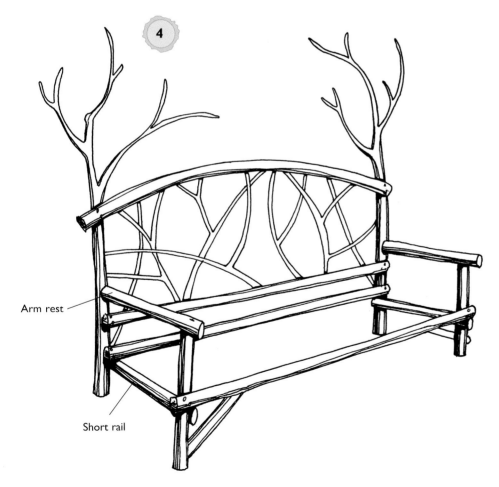

Arm rest

Short rail

Step 4: Stand the front and back frameworks upright on a flat, level surface, with the crosspieces on the inside facing each other. You will have to support them somehow while you work. If you don't have a helper, you might tie them to the wall or to your worktable.

Join the front and back assembly at each side with a 22" short rail placed just below the 16" high crosspieces. Drill pilot holes, and attach the side pieces to the legs and to the crosspieces with deck screws.

Now add arm rests on each side. You could sculpt the ends of the pieces (page 19) and butt them against the rear leg post. Secure with deck screws driven through the back of the rear leg posts and into the end of the arm rests. Secure the front of the arms with deck screws driven down through the top of the arm pieces and into the tops of the front legs.

Step 5: You can either decorate the sides with strong twigs or provide triangular bracing with strong sticks. The bench will be strongest if your bracing connects to both the arms and the 22" short rails as well as to both front and back legs.

Twig bracing

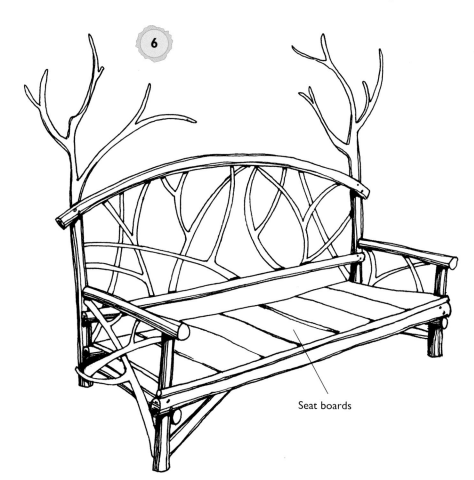

Seat boards

Step 6: Measure the distance from the back of the rear crosspiece to the middle of the front crosspiece. Create seat boards cut to this length from flat cedar boards, or from smooth branches of equal thickness. For comfort, they should be smooth on the top surface. Place the boards or sticks across the crosspieces, spaced evenly. You can fasten them from the top (an easier method, although the screw heads will show) or from below, through the crosspieces and up into the seat pieces (a classier look, but more challenging, where the screws don't show).

If you are fastening from below, once the boards are fastened securely at the front, the bench can be laid onto its back. This makes it easier to reach the back crosspiece and work from there. If you are using boards, they must be fastened with two screws at the front and two at the back (four screws per board) to prevent warping of the boards.

Add a 1"-thick trim piece to the front of the boards to finish it off.

≈ (left) This bench variation uses an eccentric top rail, deformed by clinging vines, a radiant pattern of straight branches for the back, and a curved branch in place of the diagonal braces. This bench and garden belong to Ren Moffatt and Janet Laba.

≈ (below) This bench, found outside my own workshop, is more classic in style, foregoing the towering rear legs and using vertical slats for the back.

Garden Chair

My classic garden chair is the most
challenging project in this book,
but also one of the most reward-
ing. With just a little patience, you
should find you can accomplish
this. It is commonly made with an
alder frame and the rest done in
willow, but I've also adapted it to
woods not so easily bent. If using
willow, you may want to change the
seat design to a more traditional
one. If you do use willow, select 8
to 12 long, thin, flexible willow
rods to reach from the front trim
to the back of the seat while curv-
ing up to form the back. This can
also be done with cedar, though it
can be difficult to find such long,
thin pieces, and they're not as
flexible as willow.

The seat of this chair is fairly
low—about 15 inches from the floor
compared to about 17 inches for an
average kitchen chair. With a cush-
ion, the seat height is comfortable,
but I mention this because it can be
difficult for some people to get out
of low chairs. If you want the seat
to be higher, make the front and
back legs longer.

When I teach classes on this
chair, I bring a pattern for the side
frames. It is drawn with black mark-
er on a somewhat transparent
paper, so it provides a mirror image
when turned over. With this technique, the angles and spacing are
the same on both sides of the chair.
A template like this also is handy
when you're making several chairs.

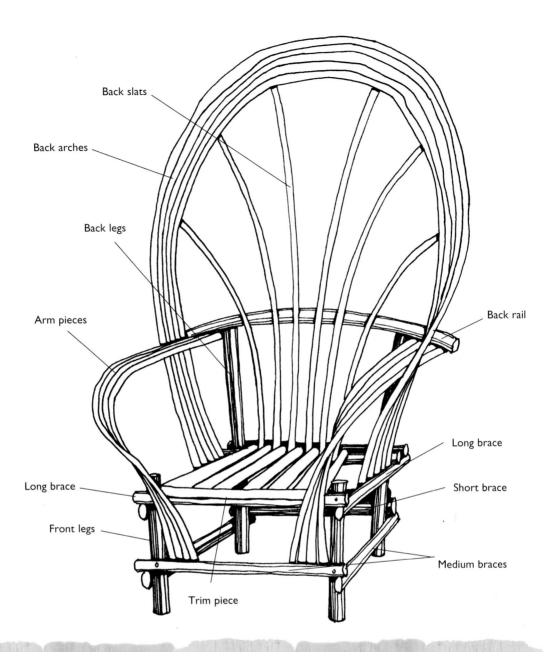

Back slats

Back arches

Back legs

Arm pieces

Long brace

Front legs

Trim piece

Back rail

Long brace

Short brace

Medium braces

Tools:

∽ Power drill
∽ Saw
∽ Pruning shears

Materials:

∽ (2) Back legs: 2" in diameter, 24" long

∽ (2) Front legs: 2" in diameter, 15" long

∽ (3) Long braces: 1½" in diameter, 24" long

∽ (5) Medium braces: 1½" diameter, 22" long

∽ (1) Short brace: 1½" in diameter, 20" long

∽ (1) Back rail: 1½" in diameter, decorative curved piece, about 30" long

∽ (2) Diagonal braces: 1" to 1½" in diameter, 24" long

∽ (8) Arm pieces: thin, flexible pieces about 1" in diameter at the base, 42 to 48" long

∽ (5) Back arches: thin, flexible pieces, 1" inch in diameter at the base

∽ (7) Seat pieces: 1" in diameter, 24" long

∽ (6 or 8) Back slats: long, curved pieces

∽ (1) Trim piece: 1" diameter, 18" long

∽ Assorted screws

Step 1: For the side frames, assemble two 24-inch back legs and two 15-inch front legs. You'll also need two 24-inch long braces and two 22-inch medium braces. Set a front and back leg on a worktable and place one long brace and one medium brace over them. These are not flush with the uprights, but extend 1" to 1½" beyond them. At each juncture, drill two pilot holes as far apart as possible. Drive a nail or heavy screw into one of the holes in each pair. Adjust the frame to a shape you like and add the second nail or screw at each juncture. Repeat to make a mirrored second frame.

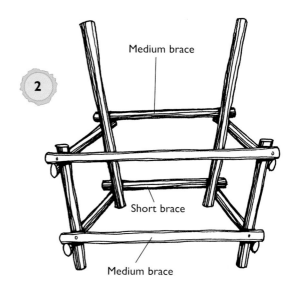

Rear leg
Front leg
Long brace
Medium brace

Step 2: Stand the frames up, with the braces on the outside. Line up the front legs with the front edge of your worktable. The back legs should be 2" closer together than the front legs. (If you were to look at a pattern made by these four posts, it would be an equal trapezoid.) The two frames will slant slightly outwards. It's tricky to hold these pieces exactly where you want them while you drill pilot holes and fasten them. Recruit a helper if you can. If not, use whatever you have to prop the pieces up and keep them in position. (When I am alone, I put them on the worktable in front of me, pushed up against the back wall, and support them with a box, bucket, or another tool.) Fit a long brace (24") against the front legs at the front, resting on the protruding ends of the side long brace. Place a medium brace (22") against the front legs resting on the protruding ends of the side medium braces. These should be in front of the front legs. (It is pleasing for this medium piece to be slightly arched as in the photo.) Rest a medium brace (22") against the back post on the protruding ends of the side long braces. Place a short brace (20") against the back post and on the protruding end of the medium braces. These should be against the back of the back legs. (As I mentioned before, the frames will angle in, becoming narrower at the back. They will also tip slightly out.) Join these pieces one at a time, with two long screws at each juncture, one going into the braces and the other going into the legs.

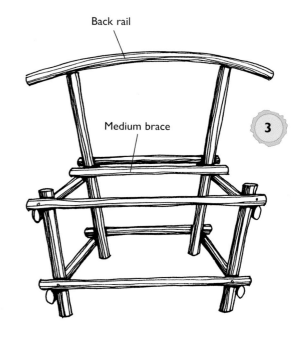

Medium brace
Short brace
Medium brace

Step 3: Place another medium brace (22") on top of the upper braces, running from one side frame to the other. (The closer this brace is to the back legs, the more upright the back will be. Place it where you will feel most comfortable.) A comfortable distance for most people would be a 1- to 2-inch gap between the crosspiece and the back legs. Drill a pilot hole and drive one long screw through this brace and into the upper side braces at each end of this medium brace.

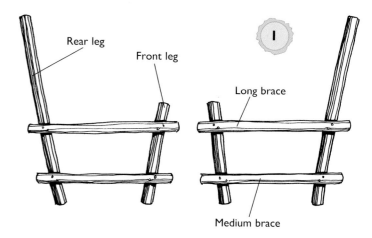

Back rail
Medium brace

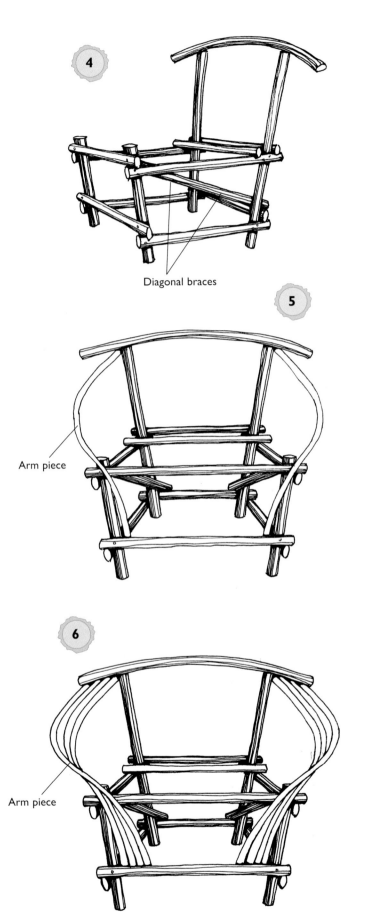

4

Diagonal braces

5

Arm piece

6

Arm piece

Next, fasten the back rail to the top of the back legs. (This arched piece needs to extend beyond the back posts about 4 inches on each side to provide support for the arm rests to come.

Step 4: Set the frame upright and make sure all four legs are touching the table. Drill pilot holes and attach two diagonal braces inside the framework, placed as shown by the dotted line in the illustration. (Occasionally there will be a twist, and one leg will seem to be a bit long or another will seem short. If this is the case, put pressure on the top of the frame as you are screwing on the braces so that all legs touch the table at the same time.)

Step 5: Choose eight thin arm pieces 42 to 48 inches long and ¾ inch to 1 inch at the heavy end. Trim them well, close to the main stem. Gently work them so that they bend easily: Place the heavy end at an angle towards the floor and put gentle pressure on it with your foot, moving up and down the length until it is more supple. (In basket-making terms, this is called "taking the spite out of it.") Place the heavy end of the first arm piece inside the lower brace at the front of the chair and to the inside of the front leg. Predrill and fasten it with a screw. Bring the branch up in line with the middle of the top of the front leg and place the thin end under the top of the back rail, so that the top of the arm is parallel to the floor. Fasten the branch with a screw going up from below, joining the thin end to the back rail. Place another branch on the other side, making sure it's about the same shape and height as the first. Trim the ends about 3 inches out from the back leg.

Step 6: Place a second arm piece inside the first one, and fasten it to the lower brace. Now bring the branch up, crossing over the first one at about half its height, carrying it along the outside of the first piece. Fasten it where necessary with short screws; put one screw under the back rail. Continue until you have four pieces on each arm. (This is a bit tricky. What you are trying to do is get an even twist to the entire arm. I explain it to my classes this way: Lay your hand across the inside of the bottom of the arm. All four pieces should lie flat against your hand. As you move your hand up along the length of the arm, the four branches should always lie flat along the same plane of your hand, while the entire arm is twisting.)

Step 7: Choose five long, thin pieces for the back arches and gently take the spite out of them (page 20) so that they will bend easily (see Step 5). Use the longest for the outside (last) piece and the second longest for the first piece. The others do not have to reach all the way across, but must at least reach from their base to the farthest arm. Place the heavy end of the second-longest piece outside of the arm and inside the upper long brace on the original side frame, right in front of the 22-inch piece across the seat. Fasten the branch with a screw, then bring it up in front of the back rail, across and down the other side, and fasten the thin end either on to the back rail or on to the upper long brace on the side frame. Make sure you have created a high, even arch. This is very important, as this first piece will dictate the shape of the others, and thus the shape of the entire back.

Step 8: Take the next back arch piece and start it on the other side of the frame (the side at which you ended the first piece). Bring the piece up in front of the first one (forward along the arm), and then above the first piece as it goes across the back, moving in front again as it comes down the side. This creates a bit of a twist in the back similar to the twist of the arms. Fasten the piece along the way as necessary. Continue with the remaining pieces, using the longest piece last.

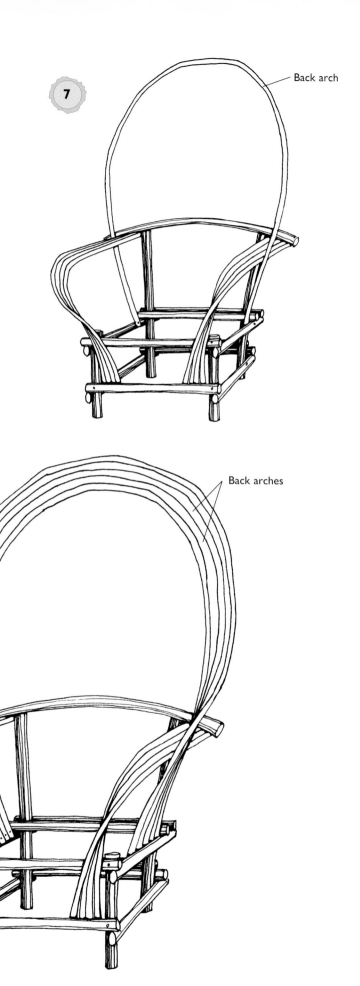

Back arch

Back arches

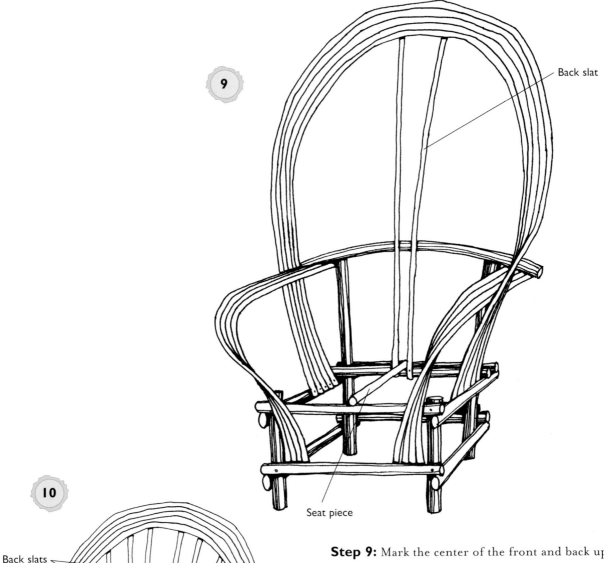

9

Back slat

Seat piece

10

Back slats

Seat pieces

Step 9: Mark the center of the front and back upper braces. Fasten a 24-inch seat piece there, about half an inch back from the edge. Now choose two straight back slats, one on each side of the seat piece. Place these behind the bent twig back, in front of the back rail and in front of the seat brace. (Fasten them onto the seat brace.) They will be spread evenly and fastened above later on.

Step 10: Place a seat piece on either side of the upright back slat, but do not fasten them yet (right now they act as spacers.) Pick two more back slats that match each other with a slight curve, and put them onto the outside of the second and third seat pieces, fastening them onto the seat braces at their bases. Proceed until there are 7 seat pieces and 6 or 8 back slats, each with more curve that the ones before. (Whether you use 6 or 8 back slats will depend on how it looks to you; however, you will always have 7 seat pieces.)

Step 11: Cut a front trim piece out of a smooth, straight stick. (It will go across the ends of the seat pieces, creating a rounded shape that will be more comfortable for the backs of your legs.) This piece is usually about 18 inches long, but it can vary, so measure to make sure the piece you select will fit. Fasten the piece to the center seat piece. Now spread your seat pieces evenly so that the outside ones are against the legs. They should all come forward to the edge of the trim piece. Turn each one so that a smooth side is up. Fasten them at the front to the top front crosspiece of the frame. Drill pilot holes and drive screws to attach the trim piece to the second and fifth seat pieces, making sure you don't hit the screws that are already in there.

Step 12: Turn the chair around so you're working on the back. (At this point you can sit down and face it, as you may be getting pretty tired. Sitting also puts you at a better working height.) Fasten all the seat pieces at the back.

Now turn your attention to the 6 or 8 back slats. Trim them with pruning shears or a saw, depending on their thickness. Spread them out so they're evenly spaced on the back support. Drill pilot holes and drive screws from through the back support, using screws that will secure the uprights without poking through them.

Note: When I first started making these chairs, I started with a central back piece and worked out from there. I thought it looked nice—more symetrical. Then someone pointed out that a chair like that wasn't comfortable because your spine hit the center piece. Removing all the bumps on the back slats also makes the chair more comfortable.

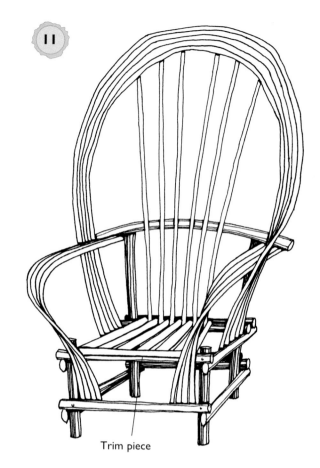

11

Trim piece

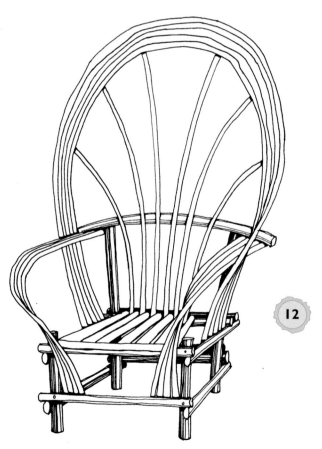

12

∾ (left) To make child-sized pieces, play with the dimensions of the side and front frames. To fit a two- to three-year-old child, I make the front posts 12 inches high, the back posts 16 inches, the tops of the sides 16 inches, and the bottoms of the sides 14 inches. I then make the front braces 16 and 14 inches, and the back braces 14 and 12 inches long.

∾ (below) To make a sofa, make the upper brace on the front 48 inches long and the lower front one 46 inches long. Make the upper brace on the back 46 inches long and the lower one 44 inches. Because these braces are quite long, you need to add bracing on both the front and the back so the frame doesn't sag when you sit on it, similar to the bracing on the garden bench. You can bring straight or arched pieces up from each leg to the back of the upper brace, or you can use decorative pieces. (Remember to leave space for the arms to be inserted at the back of the lower front brace.)

Metric Equivalents

Inches (in.)	1/64	1/32	1/25	1/16	1/8	1/4	3/8		1/2	5/8	3/4	7/8	1	2	3	4	5	6	7	8	9	10	11	12	36	39.4
Feet (ft.)																								1	3	3½
Yards (yd.)																									1	1½
Millimeters (mm)	0.40	0.79	1	1.59	3.18	6.35	9.53	10	12.7	15.9	19.1	22.2	25.4	50.8	76.2	101.6	127	152	178	203	229	254	279	305	914	1,000
Centimeters (cm)							0.95	1	1.27	1.59	1.91	2.22	2.54	5.08	7.62	10.16	12.7	15.2	17.8	20.3	22.9	25.4	27.9	30.5	91.4	100
Meters (m)																								.30	.91	1.00

Converting Measurements

TO CONVERT:	TO:	MULTIPLY BY:
Inches	Millimeters	25.4
Inches	Centimeters	2.54
Feet	Meters	0.305
Yards	Meters	0.914
Miles	Kilometers	1.609
Square inches	Square centimeters	6.45
Square feet	Square meters	0.093
Square yards	Square meters	0.836
Cubic inches	Cubic centimeters	16.4
Cubic feet	Cubic meters	0.0283
Cubic yards	Cubic meters	0.765
Pints (U.S.)	Liters	0.473 (Imp. 0.568)
Quarts (U.S.)	Liters	0.946 (Imp. 1.136)
Gallons (U.S.)	Liters	3.785 (Imp. 4.546)
Ounces	Grams	28.4
Pounds	Kilograms	0.454
Tons	Metric tons	0.907

TO CONVERT:	TO:	MULTIPLY BY:
Millimeters	Inches	0.039
Centimeters	Inches	0.394
Meters	Feet	3.28
Meters	Yards	1.09
Kilometers	Miles	0.621
Square centimeters	Square inches	0.155
Square meters	Square feet	10.8
Square meters	Square yards	1.2
Cubic centimeters	Cubic inches	0.061
Cubic meters	Cubic feet	35.3
Cubic meters	Cubic yards	1.31
Liters	Pints (U.S.)	2.114 (Imp. 1.76)
Liters	Quarts (U.S.)	1.057 (Imp. 0.88)
Liters	Gallons (U.S.)	0.264 (Imp. 0.22)
Grams	Ounces	0.035
Kilograms	Pounds	2.2
Metric tons	Tons	1.1

Nails

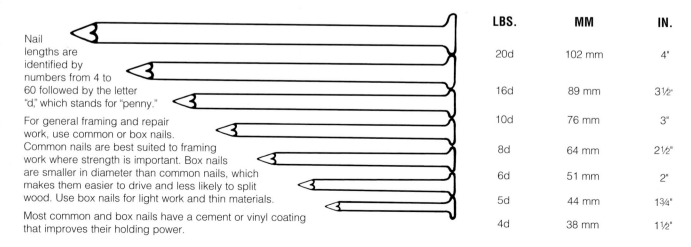

Nail lengths are identified by numbers from 4 to 60 followed by the letter "d," which stands for "penny."

For general framing and repair work, use common or box nails. Common nails are best suited to framing work where strength is important. Box nails are smaller in diameter than common nails, which makes them easier to drive and less likely to split wood. Use box nails for light work and thin materials.

Most common and box nails have a cement or vinyl coating that improves their holding power.

LBS.	MM	IN.
20d	102 mm	4"
16d	89 mm	3½"
10d	76 mm	3"
8d	64 mm	2½"
6d	51 mm	2"
5d	44 mm	1¾"
4d	38 mm	1½"

Index

Index (continued)